GUESTS OF THE THIRD REICH

Guests of the Third Reich

Anthony Richards

IMPERIAL WAR MUSEUMS

Published by IWM, Lambeth Road, London SE1 6HZ
iwm.org.uk

ISBN 978-1-912423-06-4

A catalogue record for this book is available from the British Library
Printed and bound by CPI Group (UK) LTD, Croydon, CR0 4YY

All images © IWM unless otherwise stated

Front cover: HU 47084 (artificially coloured)
Back cover: BU 3661

10 9 8 7 6 5 4 3 2 1

Contents

Preface

Modern-day perceptions of life as a prisoner of war (POW) during 1939–1945 are largely influenced by the rose-tinted filter generated by popular post-war films and television series. Movies such as *The Great Escape* (1963) and *Von Ryan's Express* (1965) focus on the daring exploits carried out by captive servicemen and tend to stress the romantic notions of courage and comradeship. Such portrayals were in turn heavily influenced by a surge of prisoner of war literature which was published shortly after the war, the key text being Pat Reid's *The Colditz Story* (1952), which again, although undoubtedly a much more accurate portrayal of prisoner of war life, still emphasised escaping as the major activity for those in German hands.

In truth, the experiences of Allied prisoners of war in Europe varied enormously according to their rank, the location of their prison camp, the time when they were captured and many other factors. While the urge to escape, coupled with the romantic notions of courage, comradeship and compassion, certainly proved to be a major part of the POW experience more often than not, we also need to recognise the even greater importance in their lives of simple hunger and boredom, constant deprivation, neglect and, sometimes, cruelty on the part of their captors. One of the prisoners whose experiences we will follow in this book is Stanley Doughty, an armoured car driver with the 7th Armoured Division who, when writing about his wartime experience in the 1990s, reflected on the importance of giving an accurate portrayal of prisoner life.

I can't say that there was much talk of escape, as there is in all the best post-war films. Men were generally in very poor physical shape, and extra exertion was difficult; we were hundreds of miles from the coast or Switzerland, and the nearest Allied troops beyond reach. Just living from one day to the next provided all the excitement and problems that most of us needed.

In writing this book, I have therefore carefully considered the balance between covering the regular, day-to-day existence of prisoners of war, which was largely one of routine and boredom, compared to the more 'exciting' incidents of escape and resistance. You will still find a significant amount here on escaping, with chapters devoted to Stalag Luft III and Colditz, the two locations most closely associated with such stories, but I have endeavoured to place these actions within the wider context of the prisoner of war experience. Even for those prisoners who never entertained the idea of escaping, stories and rumours of those who did would have inspired them throughout the boredom of captivity.

While focusing mostly on the incredible accounts of British POWs, many Commonwealth and Empire servicemen also feature. We will closely follow the experience of Australian Edgar Randolph, for instance, who fell into Russian hands at the end of the conflict. There is also a deliberate concentration on prisoner of war life in Germany, rather than Italy or the Balkans, since the vast majority of prisoners ended up in this location and the German experience could be seen as defining the others to a great extent.

Another problem faced when studying the life of prisoners of war is that each person's experience was unique and living in captivity might differ dramatically among individuals, between camps and across the span of the war. For every prisoner that enjoyed theatrical shows, another might have never heard music within their camp. For every camp with regular mail or parcels, another might have suffered from irregular deliveries or even none at all. Yet despite these differences there were many more shared experiences, which commonly reoccur in the wealth of personal testimony: the drudgery and boredom; relationships with the guards; the constant emphasis on food; and a passion felt by some to escape. I have therefore concentrated on these common themes in order to provide a study of what life was like for a typical prisoner of war, told wherever possible through the words of the men themselves.

Acknowledgements

The author would like to thank the families and copyright holders of those individuals whose experiences are included in this book, for allowing the extracts to be reproduced here. All of the quotes are taken from much longer collections of written reminiscences or transcribed from oral history recordings, held in the care of the Imperial War Museum archives. I would encourage anybody who may be interested in undertaking further research to consult these full sources. Considerable thanks must also go to David Tibbs and Madeleine James of the IWM Publishing team, with David in particular making a huge contribution to the book. Thanks also to Stephen Long for such a lovely design. Stephen Walton was also immensely helpful in providing historical advice, especially on all things German. And finally, a special thank you to Natasha and Henry, with whom I spent many happy evenings watching the BBC Colditz series.

I | Captured

I am convinced that no man living can put into words what my feelings were at that moment. What had happened?

When soldiers, sailors or airmen were captured it largely came as a significant shock. The thoughts of Private Eric Laker, captured in North Africa during the Battle of El Alamein, on 28 October 1942, were typical of servicemen who suddenly had to come to terms with a startlingly new way of life.

I am in Italy. A prisoner of war. Funny that really, because whoever I speak to agrees with me that that is the last thing that enters one's head when going into action. The thought that you may stop a fatal one occurs to you, and also that you may get wounded either more or less severely, but that you may be captured never enters your head. Maybe it is just as well.

Many prisoners struggled with real emotional trauma, coming to terms with the dishonourable reputation attached to having been forced to surrender. There was often a general sense of humiliation connected to being captured, with servicemen feeling shame at having been overwhelmed by the enemy. Many men subsequently spent their time as prisoners of war trying to resolve these thoughts in their minds, and by doing so attempted to address their personal culpability in the defeat or surrender which had changed their lives.

Around 200,000 British, Commonwealth and Empire troops were held in German or Italian hands as prisoners of war in Europe during the Second World War. This number collectively made up the vast majority of Allied prisoners of war in Europe, far outnumbering American troops in captivity, who totalled around 95,000. The United States entered the war later than her allies and her troops were involved in Europe in limited numbers prior to D-Day, while Britain had seen involvement at a much earlier stage and suffered notable defeats early on in the conflict.

Becoming a prisoner of war fundamentally changed a soldier's purpose. He was no longer in a position to be able to fight the enemy, but was rather put into a subservient situation in which he essentially became impotent as a tool of war. Many men struggled with this and did their best to continue fighting in their own way despite being in captivity, either by seeking to escape or by simply making sure that their captors' lives were made as difficult as possible. Other prisoners were more limited in their options and preferred to concentrate on getting through the experience of captivity in as painless a manner as they were able.

There was often a significant difference in immediate attitude between prisoners captured early on in the war and those who entered captivity in later years. Generally speaking, those captured in 1940 were much more likely to grow despondent with their situation than those captured after D-Day, by which time the course of the conflict had changed very clearly in the Allies' favour. In particular, soldiers who had failed to escape from Dunkirk found it difficult to come to terms with the fact that they were now out of the fight so early on in the war.

Approximately one-third of all wartime prisoners of war were captured during the Battle of France between May and June 1940, the first real battles following the period of 'Phoney War' which had been festering since the outbreak of the conflict in September 1939. Beginning on 10 May 1940, the Germans' *Blitzkrieg* attack through Belgium and France swept all before it and the French and Belgian Armies and the British Expeditionary Force (BEF) found themselves overwhelmed by the speed and ferocity of the attack. Mass evacuations from the French beaches around Dunkirk began on 26 May, but despite some 338,226 soldiers being rescued in this way, a huge number were left behind. By 3 June, when the last ships had sailed, there were still almost 45,000 British troops left in northern France. These servicemen were gradually captured by the Germans over the next few weeks, and with the final Allied resistance occurring at St Valery on 12 June, when more than 10,000 British soldiers of the 51st (Highland) Infantry Division were captured, as far as the British were concerned their immediate military involvement in Europe was over.

Ken Clarke had been part of the BEF's advance into Belgium with the 1st Battalion, Queen's Own Royal West Kent Regiment in May 1940, but had failed to join the retreat with the rest of his unit as he was tasked to stay behind to look after wounded. Swiftly rounded up by the advancing Germans, he was soon escorted back behind their lines, away from the battle zone.

We passed through deserted villages, all the inhabitants having fled from their homes to join the thousands of refugees on the roads as the German war machine rolled forward. Occasionally, if none of the guards were close at hand, it was possible to dash out of the column and into an empty house or shop for a quick look round for food. Sometimes we might be lucky enough to find a stale loaf, a few potatoes, a jar of pickles, anything edible, but often we drew a blank. The next problem was to elude the guards and dart back into the column at the right moment without being spotted. If caught, as many were, it meant the butt of a rifle across your back, a prod with a bayonet or, in some cases, a trigger happy guard would take a pot shot at you.

We were heading south-east along country roads in the direction of Lens and on that first day covered a distance of about 30 miles. We stopped for the night in a field and settled down as best we could to get a few hours much needed sleep, thankfully in the dry. Next day the pattern was similar, up early and on the road again, still marching south, now towards Douai. The sun came up as we trudged along the dusty roads, often aggravated as German army transport columns roared past on their way to the front line. Sometimes a sympathetic Frenchwoman who had not fled from her home would put a bucketful of water by the roadside and men dipped in a mess tin as they went past. Some nasty-minded guards would kick over these buckets and lash out with their rifle butts at men trying to get a drink.

In total, 44,800 men of the British Expeditionary Force were captured during this period, a very high proportion of the 142,319 men of the British armed forces who became prisoners during the entire war. These first prisoners of war would be seen as 'veterans' by 1945, having spent sometimes as long as five years in German hands.

Further Allied defeats led to more troops being taken prisoner. Germany invaded Greece and Yugoslavia in April 1941 and the Battle for Crete followed in May, which alone resulted in around 12,500 Allied troops being captured. Further prisoners were taken during the North African campaign which, until the tide turned at the Battle of El Alamein in October–November 1942, was largely characterised as a series of Axis victories. The breaking of the siege of Tobruk alone resulted in the garrison's 35,000 men being captured and these made up a large proportion of the 68,000 British and Commonwealth troops that were ultimately held in captivity in Italy. Despite fighting against and surrendering to German forces, troops captured on Italian soil such as those in North Africa became the responsibility of Italy. This remained the standard agreement among the Axis powers for how to deal with prisoners, although there were the odd exceptions; Italy also housed prisoners of war captured in Tunisia, for instance, which actually belonged to Vichy France.

Predictably, most British prisoners of war were soldiers, since the army was larger than all other services in terms of personnel. At the time of his capture on 28 October 1942, Eric Laker was serving with the 4th Battalion, Royal Sussex Regiment at El Alamein. Advancing under a smokescreen, he and his comrades took cover in a captured Italian trench around dawn and waited there as the sun slowly rose, awaiting their opportunity to move forwards.

At about 9am we received the shock of our lives. We were contentedly playing with our automatics when I looked up and saw some of our fellows climbing out of their slit trenches with their hands up! One even had a white handkerchief tied to his rifle. I blinked and then looked round. I saw a tank that had come over the ridge with others on the right of it. A fellow was sitting on the top with a nasty looking LMG [light machine gun] which he was waving around in a most unfriendly manner, and walking beside the tank was another chap with a revolver. He was waving his hands around him indicating to our fellows that they were to come to him and surrender. Then to my horror I saw a black cross on the front of the tank.

I am convinced that no man living can put into words what my feelings were at that moment. What had happened? Had our tanks been beaten back? Impossible! Had Jerry made a counter attack and broken through our companies? Question after question flashed through my mind as we sat seemingly frozen. Prisoners of war – horrible thought! Stories that I had heard of the gruesome camps and treatment of the last war that I had forgotten long since came streaming back to me with fearsome clarity. I tried to think straight, but the truth was that we were all a little dazed with the pounding we had received during the night and that morning. Slightly bomb-happy if you like.

Eric and his two companions climbed out of their trench, having first had the foresight to put on the packs containing their few possessions, and joined the crowd of British troops that were now beginning to stream towards the German lines.

The fact that we had to walk through a barrage from our own guns did not exactly help matters but we went steadily forwards – or was it backwards? We walked for what must have been about four miles. During that walk we were stopped first and asked for compasses, then a roughneck stopped us and took most of the fellows' cigarettes, and made us take off and dump our equipment but I managed to hang on to my haversack with washing tackle etc. in it. Then on we went again, incidentally all this time with no escort, finally being brought to a halt by an Italian officer. Here we were searched again and I was relieved of my knife, fork, spoon and tin opener, but luckily I had just put my watch down my sock. This time we were bundled into trucks and taken on, being dumped in the middle of nowhere by what I imagined to be some sort of HQ. We squatted here for some time, and were very agreeably surprised when our captors produced biscuits and Italian bully for us. We hung about until dusk, and it was during this time that the full realization of what had happened came over me. I nearly cried in my misery, if I had been alone I think I would have done so. I hoped desperately that our troops were still pushing and might catch up with us before the Wops could get us away. But it was a vain hope.

The nature of the war at sea meant that relatively few seamen were taken prisoner: only about 5,500 from the Royal Navy and a similar number from the Merchant Navy. Unless help happened to be close at hand, ships' crews tended to perish with their vessel. As an example, the sinking of the battlecruiser HMS *Hood* in May 1941 left only 3 survivors out of a total crew of 1,419 men. Sometimes the master or senior officer of a ship would be sought out and taken prisoner for interrogation purposes, but the rest of the crew would largely be left to fend for themselves in lifeboats. Even if German ships were inclined to take on board survivors from a sinking, the limited space available in their own vessels usually precluded this.

Captain Eric Monckton was master of the merchant ship *Empire Starling*, which on 21 November 1942 was carrying some 5,500 tons of frozen meat and general cargo across the Caribbean. When about 180 miles northeast of Barbados, the ship came under fire from the German submarine *U-163*, as recorded by Monckton in his later account of the incident.

The vessel shook violently and two blinding explosions occurred on the ship's port side. The shock to the ship threw me from the bottom steps of the ladder on to the deck, accompanied by flying pieces of wood and metal and a deluge of salt water. The ship took a sudden list to port of about 15 degrees and stayed a while at that angle. After throwing the weighted bag over the side and getting rid of all secret papers, I made for the boat deck and gave the orders for the crew to take to the boats and stand-by some ship's length astern. On reaching about 200 feet from the ship, there was another terrific explosion on the port side of the ship, as the submarine put in another torpedo to finish the ship off. In the blinding flash there was no view of the submarine, and following the explosion, we, in the lifeboats, felt a violent gust of wind and a deluge of sea water that drenched everyone in the boat. Within about two minutes after the ship had received the third torpedo, she turned quickly over to port and rolled down into the sea, with a dying hiss of steam.

At first it seemed that the crew's only chance now was to row towards the nearest land, or otherwise drift at sea until help arrived from a friendly ship. However, just as they were raising their masts and setting course for the West Indies, some 300–400 miles away, the German submarine surfaced and approached. Over the water could be heard the submarine commander calling for the British captain to make himself known. As the German crew took station at their gun, Monckton swiftly gave the order for his lifeboat to row towards them.

On getting alongside the submarine, the commander again asked for the captain and pointed to me, so that I went on board, and as soon as I had got on the conning tower, he asked me again if I was the captain and on my replying that I was, he said 'You are prisoner'. The commander could only speak broken English and of a very limited amount. I told him that there was a man in the boat that was injured and needed attention and would he allow me to go back into the boat so to attend him, but he said 'No, it is war' and ordered me down the ladder from the conning tower to the inside of the submarine. Before he ordered me down below, one of the crew had been given an order and closed behind me with a tommy gun pointed in my back, and he had asked where the chief engineer was. I told him that the chief engineer was where his torpedoes were, which of course was not true. The last I remember seeing of the boat was as he gave orders to his men on the forward deck of the submarine to cast off.

Unfortunately, Captain Monckton realised too late that he had left his overcoat behind in the lifeboat, including the valuable contents of its pockets.

Before going on the submarine I had thrown off my overcoat, which had cigarettes, matches and other useful things for the boats, my having always been prepared for such an accident with a coat loaded with those things that would be most acceptable when in a lifeboat for any length of time. I also left my prismatic binoculars and my wallet with my identity card, passports for USA and Argentina, personal photos and about 30 pounds in notes. I regret that none of these articles were ever looked after and returned to my wife, and I suppose that the money was stolen by someone of the crew in the boat and the rest of the wallet thrown away. On proceeding below into the submarine, I was interviewed by the 1st Oberleutnant – second in command of her – who questioned me as to the name of the ship, nature of cargo, last port of call, where bound and as to whether I was following a given route, kind of armament on the ship, etc. To all these questions he was only told the name of the ship, and to the rest of the questions I was sorry that I did not know, which made him a bit wild, and he could speak English and understand much better than the commander.

As Monckton would come to realise in the weeks ahead, this was only the start of a long interrogation process which would continue in earnest once they reached land. At the beginning of the war, all prisoners regardless of service had come under the control of the German High Command (*Oberkommando der Wehrmacht*, or OKW). Naval prisoners were initially held in separate compounds at Stalag X-B prisoner of war camp at Sandbostel, located in north-west Germany, until the German Navy took over responsibility for them in 1942. They were then largely concentrated in a purpose-built site at Westertimke, known as Marlag-Milag Nord. Royal Navy prisoners of war were held in two compounds at Marlag (*Marine Lager*) while merchant seaman (who were technically civilian internees, despite being treated in the same manner as prisoners of war) were kept in the larger adjacent camp, Milag (*Marine-Interniertenlager*). Still at sea and trapped in his captors' submarine, Eric Monckton would have to wait some weeks before being handed over.

I was given a pair of short trousers and a sports shirt to replace mine which were wringing wet still from the deluge of sea water after that third torpedo hit the Empire Starling. *I was given a berth-*

*bed in the officers' quarters, which also served as a dining mess
and recreation room for the commander and officers. I noticed
that when any of the crew passed through the officers' berth, they
always raised their hands in the Nazi salute. The second night
on board I was given a toothbrush, toothpaste, towel, razor and
equipment for shaving and a hair comb. These were all looted
goods from France, the markings being on the articles. The bed
allotted me was the top bed on the port side and it was a work of
art to get into same as it was close to the deckhead-rounding on
the submarine. Sleep was out of the question during the first night,
what with the strange surroundings, noises, stuffy atmosphere
and the thoughts of the previous happenings of the evening and
their disastrous results. I was allowed the run of the submarine
below, with the exception of the engine-room and the two torpedo
rooms, in which I was not allowed under any circumstances. As far
as I was concerned, there was little harm that I could have done
without grave injury to myself and little harm to the U-163. Escape
was out of the question and indeed hopeless, being in areas of such
isolation from any shipping.*

Proportionately fewer prisoners of war also originated from the air
force, with around 13,000 British and Commonwealth airmen ending
up in captivity. Around 10,000 of these were from bomber crews,
shot down while operating over enemy territory. Looking after air
force prisoners became a responsibility of the German Luftwaffe in
1940, who decided to build and control separate camps for airmen,
named Stalag Lufts (*Luftwaffe-Stammlager*). Seven such camps were
in existence by the end of the war, but the large number of airman
prisoners meant that, despite officers and NCOs being concentrated
wherever possible in Stalag Lufts, RAF prisoners were often also sent
to separate compounds within existing military camps.

The experience of being captured was rather different for airmen,
since the nature of their jobs meant that they were usually already

operating well inside enemy territory when they were shot down. Having bailed out of their stricken aircraft, they were typically found and captured while wandering lost in occupied territory or waiting, wounded, for medical attention. To many downed airmen, the arrival of authority figures to arrest them would have been rather welcome, since the alternative was often angry local civilians, all too eager to take revenge on the bomber crews who had seemingly targeted their homes and families. Flight Lieutenant Eric Williams was one of the three officers who would later successfully escape from Stalag Luft III as part of the 'Wooden Horse' plan. His journey as a prisoner of war began, however, when his Stirling bomber of No 75 Squadron RAF was shot down on a raid over Germany on the night of 17–18 December 1942.

We were briefed to bomb the 'People's Car Works' (i.e. Volkswagen), south-east of Berlin. We were to fly at low level – about 1,000 feet – and consisted of part of a force carrying out a widely scattered raid over the whole of Germany. My trade was bomb aimer and on this occasion I was in the front gun turret. After some hours flying, my navigator told me that he was not quite certain of our position and asked for a pinpoint. I was able to fix our position as some way south off track. Unfortunately we were further east than I thought and our new course took us over the centre of Hanover. We were coned by searchlights and hit by 'flak', which rendered our starboard engine unserviceable. After we had shaken off the searchlights the pilot asked me to go back and help him fly the aircraft, as she was becoming difficult to handle... We had some difficulty in flying the aircraft and could not climb above 1,000 feet... We set course for home and were nearing the Dutch border when the rear gunner reported a night fighter on our tail. We carried out some evasive action, greatly hampered by the unserviceable engine, and succeeded in losing the enemy aircraft several times. He then managed to get in a good burst which set us on fire and exploded the 'G' set in the navigation compartment. The aircraft was becoming increasingly difficult to fly and on being told by the pilot that we had no hope of continuing I ordered 'Abandon aircraft'. The pilot, who displayed great coolness throughout, told me that he could carry on while I jumped. He did this and crash landed in a lake. I afterwards met him at Dulag-Luft, none the worse for his experience. On landing, in a pine forest, I buried my parachute under some moss and taking the torch from my Mae West started to walk south in search of a road running east and west. After a short time I met the rear gunner, who had landed in a tree but was unhurt. We continued together and on finding a road running east we started for the Dutch border.

Unfortunately, Williams was picked up by the German authorities some three days later. We will revisit his experiences as a prisoner of war in a later chapter.

Although dependant on when and where they were captured, as well as the particular circumstances, most prisoners of war went through roughly the same stages before they ended up in their permanent camp. For those captured early on during the Battle of France, all ranks and nationalities were herded together and marched in columns eastwards across France and Belgium towards Germany. Sometimes improvised billets such as barns would be provided for the prisoners to sleep in at night, but at other times, particularly when large groups had been captured, they would be expected to make their own arrangements in fields. Food and water were often scarce. Treatment from the German guards, especially from the support units to whom the prisoners were handed over by the frontline troops, could be harsh and even brutal. The captors often took personal possessions from their prisoners, which despite being seen as pure and simple theft was widely accepted as part of the 'spoils of war'. At any rate, the disarmed and overpowered prisoners were in no position to refuse.

When the Allies returned to France in 1944, immediate experiences of captivity mirrored those of their comrades captured in 1940. Private Tom Tateson was serving in Normandy with a signals platoon of the 7th Battalion, Green Howards. Having landed on the beaches in the early hours of D-Day, 6 June 1944, he was captured just north of Villers Bocage a fortnight later, on 18 June.

The psychological effect of being taken prisoner is an almost complete numbing of the senses. We were lined up with our hands on our heads by men with Schmeiser automatics, and it went through my head that they might be going to shoot us out of hand. The dulling effect of anti-climax however meant that this thought simply left me with a detached feeling almost of curiosity rather than fear. From prolonged intense excitement leading to near exhaustion, we now experienced a complete lowering of the senses, even that of self-preservation. When dumping my kit I had recovered a leather writing wallet containing a photograph of Olive and her letters to me, and simply slipped this inside my battledress blouse. Now, with my hands on my head, the wallet slipped down and fell to the floor. I stooped and picked it up, in so doing risking an instant burst of fire and a quick death.

We now joined a considerable number of other prisoners. Continuing along the road in complete darkness we came to a part where pine needles lay thick on the ground, deadening our footsteps to almost complete silence. The darkness was so complete that as we marched along in single file one could hardly make out the man in front. The idea occurred to me that I could step aside, bend down on the pretext of tying my boot lace, and simply allow the column to pass, including the guarding soldiers bringing up the rear. It was a chance which demanded a snap decision and perhaps I might have got away with it. On the other hand, if I had been spotted, I should probably have been shot on the spot. The moment and the chance, if chance it was, passed and the feeling of dull resignation swept over me again.

During this early stage in a prisoner's captivity, there were often numerous opportunities for escape and in hindsight some prisoners might certainly have lived to regret not having taken the chance. But where would they have gone? Near the front line, escapers were most likely to be shot immediately, especially if they had not yet been registered as prisoners of war with the Red Cross. The moments when prisoners were captured in large numbers tended to be when the enemy had overwhelmed their positions, so the intimidating large numbers of troops would have deterred any escape attempt; indeed, there was nowhere to run to anyway. The suddenness of capture also served to induce disbelief and confusion in prisoners of war, and accounts by soldiers such as Tom Tateson of being struck dumb by the shock of having been taken captive were not uncommon.

We eventually came to some farm buildings where we were locked up for the remainder of the night in a large barn. We slept the sleep of exhaustion on the floor of the barn until wakened by shouts of 'Raus' ['Out'] by the German guards and demands for 'clocks' or, in other words, watches. Although still half asleep I thought quickly enough to slip my watch from my wrist and wrap it round my ankle under my sock, and fastened up my boot over it. I was just tying the lace when one of the guards hit me across the head, and holding out his hand demanded 'clock'. 'Nix clock,' I responded, and he passed on to gather his harvest elsewhere before his colleagues got there first.

Whether captured on the battlefield in large numbers and marched in a column, or picked up behind enemy lines and escorted by guards, a prisoner would most likely end up at a transport hub, where they would then be herded into railway carriages and taken deeper into enemy territory. Troops captured in theatres of war such as Greece or on Crete tended to be marshalled into very primitive holding camps where conditions were often extremely poor. The more fortunate stayed at these locations for only a few hours, while others might remain there for several months depending on the availability of transport to Italy, Austria or Germany. By 4 June 1940, the seventh day since his capture, Ken Clarke and his fellow BEF prisoners had been marched into Belgium and were about to be loaded onto cattle trucks for further transport.

With shouts and curses from the guards we were prodded and pushed and made to clamber aboard. Up to 80 men, some wounded, many suffering from the days of marching and lack of food, were crammed into each wagon, the doors of which were then shut and bolted. There was not enough room for us all to sit down and some had to remain standing around the sides of the wagon. Places on the floor were found for the sick and wounded. The only light and air came from a small barred grill high up on the side of the wagon and the men standing near these kept the rest informed about what was happening outside. As the train rattled and jolted along, conditions became more and more uncomfortable. Men got stiff from sitting or standing in one position but it was almost impossible to move a limb without kicking someone in the back or prodding them in the stomach. To relieve themselves men had to use a tin hat and pass it along overhead for someone near the grill to empty. The stench from so many unwashed bodies got steadily worse and the foul air in the wagons increased as little fresh air was able to get in. Hunger was acute… in general most of us had not eaten a proper meal for about ten days.

The train rattled on for mile after mile and as it got dark we tried to settle down and get some sleep. After a few hours those standing changed over with those sitting on the floor but there was very little sleep for anyone. The moans and cries of men in pain went on throughout the night, despite the efforts of others to comfort them. The stench increased as men with dysentery could contain themselves no longer and many were sick. Morning came at last and eventually the train pulled into a siding and stopped. After much shouting of orders the guards came along the track and undid the doors of the wagons to allow us to get out for a brief respite from the cramped conditions. We were able to give a little help to some of the sick by collecting water from the water tower while the engine was being filled up. One or two men took the opportunity to make an escape bid and dashed across the tracks in an effort to reach nearby woods. Much shouting followed by rifle shots brought the escape attempt to an end and we heard that one man had been shot as we were herded back on to the train.

Having been revived slightly by the fresh air and water, the prisoners continued their journey in somewhat better spirits. Yet this was not to last, since their status as prisoners of war was to become all too clear. Taking his turn to stand by the wagon's small window, Clarke could read the headline on a newspaper billboard as the train paused at a station. It read *'Dunkirchen ist Gefallen'* ['Dunkirk has fallen'], which did little to improve their morale.

Moving on again on our fourth day locked in the cattle trucks we were travelling across southern Germany following the course of the Moselle River, finally stopping in the town of Trier. With the usual shouting, prodding and pushing of our guards we alighted from the wagons and were formed up into some sort of order and marched out of the siding into the town. Almost every building, houses, shops and factories were decked with huge streaming red flags with a white circle in the centre containing the black Nazi swastika. It seemed as if the whole town had turned out to line the streets as we shambled past. Blackshirts, Brownshirts, Hitler Youth, Labour Corps, SS, Police, Women's and Girls' organisations as well as civilians were all there on the pavements to shout 'Heil Hitler' and give the Nazi salute as we passed. Some shouted abuse at us – English swine – some spat and raised their fists at us. Some reception! 'England kaput' was repeated many times. We must have looked a sorry sight. After three weeks in action in Belgium and France, days of marching across France after our capture, unwashed, unshaven, filthy dirty, weak from starvation and our recent ordeal in cattle wagons, and these arrogant Nazis could only laugh and shout 'England kaput'.

It was now that the beginnings of depression would often show themselves, as the prisoners of war had time to reflect on their new situation and came to realise the true implications of their predicament. Eric Monckton was particularly unfortunate in this regard, as he remained captive in the German submarine which had picked him up.

Day after day passed without any vessel coming in sight, for me a most wearying and inactive time, and I did not take to this inactivity at all kindly. Thoughts of my misfortune and failure to have got home safely with the very precious cargo that the Empire Starling *had on board; also that, from now onwards, I was of no effective use to the country and the war effort. I also worried very much over how my wife would take the news that would be sent her, if the crew eventually made land in the lifeboats and there was every possibility that they would do so in the course of a week at most. She would, of course, have to suffer in her mode of living, as an ungrateful government would ungratefully hand her a much lesser allowance of living money than I had allowed her. It made one think that the war effort was a very one sided affair with the balance on the part of the few top members of government. I found out eventually that the British government was the only one that reduced the allowances of the Merchant Seamen when they were taken prisoner.*

Corporal W G Harvey was serving at Tobruk when he was captured in June 1942. Notions of comradeship kept him going.

I suppose we were still in a state of shock, to find ourselves POW after the pride of being a worthwhile army unit and all within about four weeks. The general uncertainty of not knowing what lay in store for us and how long we should be in this unwanted capacity. One comforting thought was that we were still more or less together and we could sit or walk yearning of things at home.

Eric Laker had a long journey to make before reaching his permanent camp. Captured at El Alamein, he would first be transported to the port of Tripoli, from where the prisoners could then embark on ships across the Mediterranean to Italy. Living conditions for the men during the journey were basic to say the least, with each man reliant on whatever clothing he happened to be wearing when captured.

We were just hauled off the trucks [at night] and lay down on the ground. I was fortunate enough to have my gas cape in my haversack, but even so it was so bitterly cold that sleep was practically impossible. I was dressed in battle dress trousers, shirt and pullover – too hot in the day time but horribly insufficient at night.

Biscuits and bully beef, with rare instances of bread and coffee, were the only sustenance given to the prisoners.

That stretch of the journey from Benghazi to Tripoli was the most horrible and uncomfortable of a journey that was altogether nightmarish. To see the fellows fighting for bad biscuits, green with mildew, which had been thrown away by the Wops, was a horrible sight. A man has to be hungry before he does that. Before very long I was glad enough to eat them myself – and be thankful for them.

The vast majority of prisoners captured during the North African campaigns were from the Army. Being transferred to camps in Italy meant undergoing the highly uncomfortable and dangerous crossing across the Mediterranean to mainland Europe. In August 1942, some 432 prisoners of war had lost their lives when 2 Italian transport ships were attacked by a British submarine, so a sense of danger would have been ever-present in the minds of those making a similar crossing. Boarding his ship, Eric Laker would be transported to Palermo, in Sicily, where his journey to mainland Italy would continue.

The beginning of the most revolting and uncomfortable journey it has ever fallen to my lot to experience... 462 men were crammed down into our hold which was absolutely bare of every and any sort of fitting. We just squatted on the iron flooring, although I was lucky enough to get against the side. The fact that the hold had been used for transporting coal just made it more ideal for us in the eyes of the Italians. So much for the discomfort. The revolting part I will simply describe by saying that many men were sea sick and a large number suffering from dysentery, and leave whoever may read this to imagine the rest. Another little item was that the place was literally teeming with lice which of course fastened themselves onto all and sundry, and to this day still live and thrive on us in spite of all efforts to get rid of them, and no doubt will do so until we are released and free from this confounded country.

Even once they had arrived within Italy or Germany, the transportation of prisoners was far from a comfortable experience. Ken Clarke reflected on the horrendous conditions he continued to experience as he was transported deeper into Germany in a railway wagon.

The level of degradation to which we had been reduced in just about ten days was unbelievable. Desperate for something to smoke we had picked up cigarette ends from the gutters as we marched along and dropped them into our jacket pockets. Now, locked in the trucks, we turned out our pockets and emptied out the collection of tobacco mixed with fluff and other bits of assorted debris that

[19]

had accumulated there. Paper was at a premium and anyone with a bit of newspaper, toilet paper was favourite. Even pages from a soldier's pay book were used to roll up the mixture into cigarette shape. When lit, these were passed around as many as half a dozen men, each having a couple of puffs before passing it on.

One of the locations on the typical prisoner's journey would be a transit camp, for sorting. In Germany, most prisoners would pass through a Dulag (*Durchgangslager*), which were transit camps which not only operated as collection points for prisoners, but also served as intelligence collection centres. Dulag Lufts (*Durchgangslager der Luftwaffe*) were transit camps for air force prisoners, the main one being at Oberursel near Frankfurt. Interrogation efforts at these locations were concentrated on officers and RAF personnel, since these men were deemed to be the most likely to know any worthwhile operational secrets. Eric Williams described his arrival at Dulag Luft.

I was searched by a Feldwebel *[a German sergeant] who was very thorough, making me strip to the skin and going through every article of clothing with care. He then gave me a Polish tunic and breeches, taking my own as he said to be x-rayed. I managed to retain the silk maps and compass from the escape kit. After the search I was locked in a cell three metres by two metres and kept there for nine days. The window was of obscured glass protected by iron bars and throughout the nine days was never open. I protested but with no result. My guard expected me to sweep out my own cell but I refused. I repeatedly asked to see an officer, but was not allowed to do so for two days. When at length an officer appeared to interrogate me I asked for cigarettes, a book, exercise and a bath, but was refused all these unless I would give my squadron number, bomb load and target. I of course refused and the officer walked off, saying that he would come back in a day or two to see if I had changed my mind.*

Another officer who underwent the Dulag Luft interrogation process was Flying Officer Oliver Philpot, captured after his Beaufort aircraft was shot down off the coast of Norway in November 1941.

The first stage of Dulag treatment is solitary confinement. This adds to the already urgent desire to talk English with someone. The average man who has been shot down is already in a very shocked condition and this is often quite evident for days or even weeks after the Dulag stage. The symptoms are a general restlessness and an overwhelming desire to talk. Obviously one thing is uppermost in his mind and that is air operations. Thus when an interrogator comes in and speaks to him in English he is almost welcome, although known to represent the enemy. The prisoner in the cell then checks himself, making a mental note not to speak of air operations, but, if he is unwise, may succumb to the temptation to talk on seemingly innocuous subjects and then of course it is only a matter of time before something slips out. The whole thing is like a member of the audience going on to the stage to try and show up the 'Amazing Giovanni'. The conjuror wins every time.

Eric Williams was interrogated by three people in all, each adopting a different approach, and he later classified them in the following way.

(a) Bogus Red Cross Representative. This man had a form which he wanted me to fill in. The form started off perfectly innocently with name, date of birth, mother's and father's name, whether dead or alive, and such like personal questions, but gradually led on to date of joining RAF, where trained, for how long, where stationed, station commander's name, etc. The whole form was rather cunningly done and might easily lead one on to say more than one should. When I ran my pencil through the form and handed it back, the 'Red Cross' man lost his temper. I imagine that he had experienced this reception too often for him to see it as a joke. He informed me that unless I filled in the form my people would not know that I was a prisoner.

(b) Operational Type. This officer told me that he was an operational pilot on rest. He tried to gain my confidence by telling me that he was not an intelligence man and was just doing the job. His attitude was 'knights of the air' and he did not carry paper and pencil, but continually tried to lead the conversation round to my target. He told me that one of my crew had already told him all he wanted to know and when I told him that I did not for a minute believe him he said that I was a stupid man. On his next visit he produced a printed book containing the names of a lot of stations in England and told me that we were from Newmarket. I told him that if that was what he thought I was quite content.

(c) Confidential Type. This man I consider to be the most dangerous. He would talk for a long time on social matters, on art, national characteristics and of how Germany did not hate the English but were surprised and hurt when we declared war. He, also, did not produce paper and pencil or attempt to interrogate me. His line was that the interrogators and interpreters were university professors who had copious forms and reports which they had to fill in. He said, 'It's all red tape, you know, just a matter of form. Just tell me what they want to know. They will then lock the form away and be happy. Then you can go. There is too much form-filling in Germany, but these chaps have single track minds and I'm afraid they will not pass you through until all their nice little forms are completely filled.'

During the whole time I was in the cell I had no exercise or fresh air and nothing to read or smoke. My diet consisted of two thin slices of bread, one dry and one thinly smeared with some sort of spread, and ersatz coffee for breakfast; a plate of thin soup for lunch; and the 'breakfast' again for supper. The cell was intolerably hot, the heating being controlled from outside the cell. When I complained the guard turned the heat on still more.

Based on his own experience, Philpot could offer advice to other airmen in case they too were to undergo the same interrogation process.

In spite of the usual care, things are still from time to time found in the pockets of aircrews. Mess bills and letters are the chief offenders. After the solitary confinement treatment the prisoner is given the freedom of a compound with numerous others from the RAF. Here again the temptation to talk flying shop is practically overwhelming. The dangers of talk in the compound are: a possibly pro-German 'permanent staff' of RAF personnel, Germans 'planted' as aircrew amongst aircrew, and microphones.

Being in solitary confinement was a bad enough experience for most captured officers, yet the added insult of minimal exercise, an extremely low diet, a handful of cigarettes daily (at a time when smoking was the most common pastime) and sometimes even an absence of books, writing materials or even a pack of cards to while away the time, made the experience interminable. Under such circumstances, it was all too easy for the captives to suffer depression and feel demoralised. As one captured officer remarked, they had absolutely nothing to do, but all day to do it. The only opportunity open to them was to think, and most of the thinking would have been incredibly depressing. For many, the worst thought of all was that their family and friends back home would be unaware of their current circumstances, likely considering them killed in action.

Prisoners from other services suffered similar experiences to these airmen. As a naval officer Eric Monckton was destined for the naval Dulag at Wilhelmshaven, but first had to embark from the German submarine which had finally arrived at its base in Lorient, Brittany.

For myself, I had nothing to pack except my rotten shaving kit and some 150 cigarettes that had been handed to me… then I would be bound for this famous Merchant Navy camp, where the Nazi liars on board had told me there were golf courses and plenty of enjoyment until the war ended. The doctor and the commander had previously given me their addresses and told me that if there was anything that they could do they would welcome a letter from me. What a hope, and I could see the Gestapo allowing me to write to one of their officers in the senior service. Those addresses were quickly consigned overboard when they were not about, as they would be the very last persons in the world that were likely to receive any news from me. On my last talk with the Corvette Capitan [sic] Englemann – the commander – I told him that I was very sorry to leave his submarine for one reason and one reason only, for his sake and all the crew, as every ship I had left in the last few years had always come to grief. He turned white at the gills when this was translated to him by the lieutenant.

Back on land, Eric was taken for interrogation.

I was interviewed by a Gestapo officer, who spoke English fluently, and said that he had lived in London for some ten years or so, his job now being that of an interrogator and Nazi propaganda official. He was detailed to interview prisoners and I suppose gain all the information possible. Outside was a motor van with recording apparatus for recording speeches and talks on records. This Nazi official asked me if I cared to send a message to my wife and assured me that, after being censured in Berlin, it would be relayed over Radio Calais to England and within a fortnight. As it was the first opportunity of my wife knowing I was safe so far, since about early December, I told him that I would like a recording if it would be sent, but I much doubted if it would, as I had no faith in his promise. On his starting the recording, he commenced asking about my passage on the submarine and that he was sure that I much preferred being safe on the submarine rather than in peril in the ship's boats. I realised that this was propaganda stuff and just told him what I thought of his underwater craft and her crew as well. It was promptly cut off and, of course, the recording never sent, but the record destroyed no doubt.

The experiences of a prisoner of war were governed, at least in theory, by the Geneva Conventions of 1929. These agreements had been signed by most nations across the world with the notable exception of the Soviet Union, and their terms applied throughout western Europe. Their overall purpose was to ensure that all prisoners were treated humanely, with the requisites of the Conventions dictating how prisoners held in Germany and Italy were largely treated throughout the war. Prisoners had the right to refuse any detailed interrogation, were allowed to keep their clothing and any personal possessions (other than weapons, equipment or service papers), had the right to correspond with their families and to receive post including food, books and clothing, and should be allowed to practise their chosen religion. Rations were to be at least as good as that issued to their captor's depot troops. Prisoner of war camps were to be fixed locations away from any fighting and contain a medical facility and sanitary arrangements at least as comparable to the holding power's standard barracks.

Tom Tateson had been captured in the weeks following D-Day, when the German Army were now on the defensive in western Europe. The interrogation he received was therefore somewhat different than what might have been the case in earlier years.

My interrogator was a German soldier, the equivalent of a lance corporal. Surprisingly, he looked Jewish and spoke English with a slight cockney accent. He must have lived in England for some years, and in spite of his apparent Jewish origins was considered useful as an interpreter. His manner was subdued and in no way hostile. He simply asked for personal details and then said quietly that he envied me. 'Why's that?' I asked. 'Well,' he said, 'for you the war is over, for me – well Germany is kaput, finished.'

The relationship between captor and prisoner was a key aspect of the Geneva Conventions. Pay appropriate to rank was to be issued by the captive power, with additional pay issued for any work or physical labour undertaken. Officer prisoners were expected to salute their equals and seniors in the holding power's forces. They could not be forced to work, while warrant officers and NCOs were only allowed to supervise labour. No prisoner should be given dangerous work or have to undertake anything in such amounts which might impinge on his health. For those nationalities such as the Soviet Union who had not signed up to the Conventions, there was little to prevent the harsh treatment regularly doled out by their German captors, as could be attested by Ken Clarke.

One day I saw a Russian prisoner, who looked no more than skin and bone, collapse as he tried to dig a trench. He was immediately kicked and shouted at to get up and get on with his work. When he failed to respond the German guard cold-bloodedly took his rifle from his shoulder and shot the man as he lay on the ground. This treatment of the Russian prisoners was commonplace and sickened the British POWs who were powerless to do anything about it.

Prisoners of war had already usually been sorted into groups separated by nationality, service and rank before arrival at their transit camp in Italy or Germany. Camps in both countries distinguished between officers and other ranks, but in Italy were identified by numbers and the prefix 'Campo P.G.' (*Campo Prigioniero di Guerra* or 'Prisoner of War Camp'). Officer prisoners in Germany were sent to Oflags (*Offizierslager*). Non-officer prisoners in Germany, who according to the Geneva Conventions were entitled to work for their captors, were sent to Stalags (*Stammlager*) or smaller Labour Camps attached to them (*Arbeitskommandos*). Non-commissioned officers might end up at either location but were usually sent to a Stalag, as they were not permitted to work but could be asked to supervise labour. Any such toil undertaken by prisoners of war was not supposed to have a direct connection to the war effort, but the Germans were not overly concerned in enforcing what was admittedly a rather difficult criterion to meet.

Shortly after the Battle for France in 1940, Ken Clarke and his comrades finally arrived at their final destination, which was the permanent camp of Stalag XXI-A, located at Schildberg in Poland.

Here we were fingerprinted and had to give details of our name, rank and army number, nationality, date of birth, religion, occupation and home address. We were then photographed, holding a slate in front of us on which had been written the POW number which we had been allocated, in my case No 1001. A metal tag on a length of string was handed to us showing the camp designation, Stalag XXI-A, the words 'Kriegsgefangener' [prisoner of war] and our POW number. These we were ordered to wear around our necks at all times and failure to do so would be considered a serious offence.

Basic information such as next of kin, home address and distinguishing features were all noted. Sometimes a prisoner's ethnicity was questioned, with strict Nazi officials keen to discriminate against Jewish servicemen or others deemed to be 'racially inferior'. Sometimes Jewish servicemen would feel pressured to claim alternative religious belief in order to ensure that they remained with their comrades. Then there usually followed the delousing process, in which a prisoner's body hair was shaved off before they showered with antiseptic soap, their clothing being fumigated to get rid of any lice. Lice carried the deadly disease of typhus and so the requirement of good hygiene was considered very important when so many bodies were living together in a confined space. There were always exceptions to the rule, however, and Captain Eric Monckton would provide a perfect example of how certain prisoners received a rather unique reception by their captors. He had been transported by train to the naval Dulag at Wilhelmshaven, arriving there on 9 January 1943.

We were each issued with three blankets, one white sheet, one pillow case, knife, fork, spoon, brown enamel bowl and a small tablet of ersatz soap which had to last us for a month. We were all then separated and I was escorted to the top floor and placed in a large attic room, which I was in for four days on my own. The only daylight was through a slanting window in the lower part of the roof. The place was alive with rats and they were provided with a fine nesting-place in the spare straw beds that were heaped on the ten beds arranged two in height in the room. I learned later that this building had been the Naval Cadets Training College, was 50 years old and had not been used as a college for some considerable time. During the Hitler regime it had been used as a jail for prisoners awaiting trial for offences against the Hitler Party and I expect many a poor wretch had eventually been taken out from here to face his last few hours on earth.

After spending several days in my attic room I was taken out and placed in another room on the second floor, the floor below the attic, and I was glad in a way as sleep was out of the question at night-time what with the rats gnawing and prancing about. They ate most of my food that I had placed by to eat if I got really ravenous. A large window looked down on to a road passing from Wilhelmshaven to the riverside. The view from the window was well impressed on my memory as that view was all I had, except once, for the two months I was imprisoned in this jail. I spent about one and a half months in solitary confinement in this room on the second floor of the jail, only being out of the room for the half hour exercise, if the weather was fine, and once a week instead of the exercise to go to the wash-house for a bath and to wash out my underclothes.

Eric took the opportunity to complain to the authorities about his harsh treatment, with mixed results. The memoir he wrote after the war reveals such harsh criticism of the Nazi regime that it is tempting to think that his rebellious attitude gained him a reputation of being a 'difficult' prisoner, which in turn might explain why he was to remain in solitary confinement for much longer than was the usual arrangement.

At this bath-house was a rat-faced orderly, a Nazi private soldier and about the nastiest piece of work that this earth could produce. His appearance was enough to put one off a bath, a consumptive looking creature with only two tusks of teeth in his mouth and deformed in one leg. His attitude to all prisoners was antagonistic and he delighted in cutting off the warm shower bath water when one had just completed soaping oneself, not giving anyone the chance of swilling the soapy water off. This disagreeable soap was of a chalky nature and left always a white scum after any wash, so the results of a bath without properly swilling off were very uncomfortable. After having several baths and standing this devil's caper as long as I could, I refused to go to the bath when one day the guard came to escort me. I asked to see the Prison Commandant and eventually an officer came to see what the trouble was about. I told him what I thought of his jail and the rotten treatment that was meted out to the prisoners and that, if the opportunity ever occurred to be able to report to the Red Cross about it, I certainly would. I did not get my bath that week, and next week when I was called to go to the bathroom place, I thought I would give it a trial and see if anything had happened in the matter. I was treated with scowls from the devilish attendant, but there was no shouting at me or being chased away when only half washed.

I had been in trouble before this, when a bucket of cold water and a mop had been pushed in the opened door, for me to clean out the floor of the room. I had kicked the bucket and mop out into the corridor and the guard had given out a torrent of abuse in German, and brought up the German prison officer on duty. I told him that I did not come to Germany to be a housemaid, and that as he knew that in the German service they always respected their merchant commanders, I demanded a similar treatment. Ever afterwards a German rating did the room out twice a week. Maybe that these incidents did not do me any good, but I was not going to be treated as a dog and did not care much if the dust in my room mounted to inches in height, as I certainly had no intention of cleaning their lousy Nazi jail for them. Perhaps these, and other things that occurred, were the means of my being kept in this jail so long, for I checked up later on at the camp and found that officers and captains had been brought to this place and after only a few days or weeks had been sent to the Merchant Navy camp farther east.

After a stay of perhaps a week or two at a German Dulag or Italian transit camp, the average prisoner would then be transferred, perhaps via further holding locations, to their permanent prisoner of war camp. At the start of the war, Germany had 31 such camps. By the end of the war, this had risen to a massive 248 camps, of which 134 housed British and American prisoners. At its peak, Italy operated 72. Permanent camps in both Germany and Italy varied quite a bit in nature, depending on their location, purpose and history. While many Stalags in Germany were purpose-built prison camps, many others adapted existing buildings which were previously in use as schools, barracks or castles. Colditz Castle is one of the best-known German examples, but Italy followed this practise too, as in the case of Vincigliata Castle near Florence. German camps were arranged and numbered by military district, with each district designated by a Roman numeral. A letter following the Roman number marked individual camps, so Oflag IV-C was the third Oflag in military district IV, which happened to be Dresden. Sub-camps were given a suffix '/Z' (*Zweiglager* or sub-camp) while the main camp had a suffix of '/H' (*Hauptlager* or main camp). The administrative language extended to the prisoners themselves, who in Germany were known as *Kriegsgefangenen* or 'Kriegies'.

Arrival at their proper camps would provide for many prisoners the first opportunity in many weeks or months to shelve their itinerant lifestyle and begin to establish their new mode of existence. They would have to adapt to an alternative way of living which would be based on necessity and hardship, and for many this might equate to as long as four or five years of uninterrupted captivity.

2 | Life in Captivity

All day today I have been feeling fed up, miserable and very homesick

If prisoner of war life began with capture, interrogation, classification and transport, the next stage of captivity would be arrival at a permanent camp. It would be here that a prisoner would usually spend the remainder of his time in captivity, living and interacting with other prisoners and becoming part of a new community based on the necessities of captivity. Prisoners soon had to come to terms with this new environment. Each man now found himself in a foreign country well behind enemy lines, his movements restricted to a small area, with limited resources to feed, clothe and look after himself. He would also be experiencing great uncertainty over the future. Every man would now be completely reliant on his captors for safety and sustenance, and would need to get along with other prisoners as best he could in order to survive the experience. And as all would eventually find out, the overwhelming characteristic of prisoner of war life was simple boredom. Spending most of one's time hungry meant that prisoners would become fixated on when their next meal would arrive, while their thoughts might similarly dwell on the absence of news from home, leading to an obsession with when the next mail would be delivered to their camp.

Monotony was not always such a defining factor, of course, since work camps ensured that prisoners were kept occupied on labour and any spare time was consequently spent resting or asleep, but the vast majority of prisoners found that they suddenly had a lot of spare time to fill. Officers in particular, forbidden to work by the Geneva Conventions, had more 'free time' than most. The way that the majority of men coped with this boredom was to keep themselves busy and try to lead as organised a life as far as possible under the circumstances, arranging their own recreational activities whether it was sport, theatre, educational classes or gardening. For some, amusement might extend to 'goon baiting', which involved poking fun at the guards and making their lives a general misery. Others would concentrate their efforts on devising ways to escape.

In late 1944, Tom Tateson arrived at Stalag IV-B, near Mühlberg in Saxony, where he was astounded at the impressive conditions evident in a permanent camp as compared to the transit camps he had previously experienced.

We seemed suddenly to be back in civilization, and could hardly believe our eyes. In the first place we were shown to our accommodation huts which contained single tier beds reasonably spaced, and supplied with a row of well-spaced beds (not bunk beds) on each side. We were told to leave our scanty possessions on our beds. The possessions consisted of Red Cross boxes containing perhaps a few bits of food, old personal letters, shaving kit and toothbrush, a 'hussif' (the army issue sewing and darning kit), an empty tin for use as a drinking vessel, and in some cases, cigarettes. These had until now been carried about with us at all times, slung over the shoulder with a piece of string. The suggestion that they should now be left unguarded on our beds seemed horrendous. However, we were left in no doubt by the British NCOs now in charge of us that this was an order. No-one would be allowed to walk around carrying his precious box and there would be no thieving. Incredibly this proved to be true; nothing was stolen – everyone was on trust and had trust in everyone else.

Once established and freed from our burdens, we wandered over the camp, astonished at every turn. The first thing I came across was a football match in progress between 'Sheffield United' and 'Tottenham Hotspur'. The football pitch was surrounded by banking for the spectators. The effect was of a well-established community, by contrast with the semi-nomadic life we had become used to. There was a notice board showing the football league tables with most of the well-known national teams represented. I learned that some of the players were in fact professional footballers and that the standard of play was very high. I next found the camp theatre with a box office of, to me, quite incredible magnificence. Tin plate from empty food tins had been used to simulate chromium plate in the façade of the box office, and lettering of professional perfection advertised that evening's performance. The camp shop was my next subject for wonderment. Neatly arranged in the window was a display of tins of Spam, bully beef, Klim, chocolate, cigarettes, etc., with a display board quoting prices of individual items in terms of cigarettes. At this length of time I am not sure whether a tin of bully beef was priced at twenty or forty cigarettes, with other items in descending order from this figure. I went to the theatre that evening to see a very competent, and to me in the circumstances, astonishingly professional performance with the female parts played by men, with no 'camp' or burlesque effect. This sudden transformation into a civilized world created a feeling of sheer luxury, no doubt very far removed from the feelings of the men who had been there for years. It was, however, a very short lived experience, since as a mere private I was destined to be sent to a working camp.

Tateson's introduction as a non-commissioned prisoner to organised labour would prove to be a rude awakening after his initial enthusiastic arrival. As he himself recognised, prisoners who had been in captivity for some time would have felt differently to more recent arrivals, although regular interaction with each other as part of a community helped to maintain morale and prevent dangerous introspection developing. Even the exchange of war news and rumours could keep minds active, as evidenced by these three diary entries from Eric Laker. Not all war rumours would prove to be entirely accurate.

Some great rumours are in circulation this morning attributed to two RAF men who are supposed to have come in last night and who were in England four days ago. 'We will be out of here in a month – war over in eight weeks – the Russians fighting in Poland' etc. We shall see anyway, but they all keep us cheerful and make something to talk about.

*

Four hundred prisoners came in last night from Capua, and gave us the following news, purporting to have been heard on the English radio. Finland and Hungary had packed in – Germany lost 3 armies retreating from Stalingrad – Russia had just thrown in a new army completely equipped – the Germans had been completely driven from the Caucasus and were losing men at the rate of 15,000 per day, and planes 50 per day. Well, time I suppose will tell if they are correct but I certainly hope and pray so.

*

10 February 1943. A terrific buzz today is that there has been an invasion of the continent between Calais and Boulogne, tanks, artillery and supplies being landed, 23,000 Huns killed, 100 planes destroyed, and we supposed to have lost many planes and men. I wonder. If these stories are not true, I wonder what pleasure people can get out of starting them.

The organisation of the camp itself helped in regard to generating a sense of community spirit. Lieutenant Commander Billie Stephens had arrived at the Royal Navy compound at Marlag-Milag Nord shortly after his capture in March 1942, and was very impressed by the reception which greeted him. Supplies and resources such as clothing and cigarettes were shared out among the prisoners there, with some so eager to assist new arrivals that they might quite literally give the shirt from off their own backs. The contents of parcels were also commonly shared out, although a minority took advantage of shortages in order to line their own pockets by selling cigarettes, food, clothing or anything else that they could get their hands on. Prices for such goods would sometimes be fantastic. The prisoners were paid by the Germans with paper money known as Lagergeld or camp marks. This currency was ineffective in the long-term unless one could save a large enough amount, but each camp's black market dealt largely in this currency and the uniquely POW currency of cigarettes.

Each camp had its own German Commandant, with on average one guard allocated for every seven to ten prisoners. Stalag Lufts holding high-value RAF prisoners or top security prisons containing troublesome inmates were felt to endure more of an escape risk, so in those cases it was often one guard for every four prisoners. Each camp had its own internal hierarchy among the prisoners too, with a Senior British Officer (SBO) in Oflags or Stalag Lufts who was usually the officer of highest rank, or a Camp Leader in Stalags elected by democratic vote. Sometimes there was also a Man of Confidence (*Vertrauensmann*), who served as a liaison officer with the Italians or Germans over matters such as rations or living conditions, and in this respect would work closely with the SBO or Camp Leader. There might also quite possibly be a secret Escape Committee to oversee and coordinate escape attempts from the camp, with the leader generally referred to as 'X'. As Eric Monckton came to realise, there was a certain hierarchy among prisoners, which was sometimes reflected by the clothing and food allocated amongst them. At the beginning of March 1943, Monckton had finally been transferred from Wilhelmshaven to the Merchant Navy compound at Marlag-Milag Nord.

The clothing situation was really bad and even though the prisoners that held the positions of being in charge of the stores, such as Camp Captain, Red Cross Clothing Officer, Postmaster, and all workers in those departments had several good Red Cross suits, I did not get one until I was in the camp for over a month. It appeared to me that to get the best and plenty of everything, one had to 'be in the racket' and get a position of trust. I went on parades with my old canvas suit for well over a month, and it was mighty cold with wind and sometimes snow lying deep on the ground. It made me very bitter to think that those in affluence had several good Red Cross suits and yet I, a fellow countryman in distress, could shiver my carcass out for all that they cared. It was very apparent that there were numerous 'racket' stunts going on in the camp and to get 'well in' with the camp management was the thing desired. One could always be assured of being well clothed, better food and abode in 'Park Lane', a barrack of rooms near the main gate, three persons on an average to each room and the room containing single iron bedsteads, nice wood-backed chairs, plenty of fuel for the room stove, and every opportunity to exchange the Nazi-desired Red Cross things out of their parcels for eggs, meat, milk, etc. that the guards could obtain from the farms around.

We will look at the importance attached to Red Cross food and clothing parcels in the following chapter, but Monckton clearly held the camp leadership in low esteem and consequently preferred to organise his meals at a more local level.

There was no need for anyone who was on the camp management to feed at the communal mess hall, which held about 600 persons, for they had ample chance to get the titbits from the hospital galley and to feed on their own in their rooms. Those who fed in the community hall had certain articles taken out of their Red Cross parcels, such products as: tinned meats, raisins, prunes, tins of fish, porridge, and about every third week the tin of milk. From these products and the meagre things the Nazis issued, the community feeding was carried on, and they gave a fair measure of food twice a day from that supply. It was at the option of the prisoner whether he partook of this communal feeding or took the whole of his Red Cross parcel and feed himself or in conjunction with any number of fellow prisoners. I started off with joining in the communal feeding but later on I joined with Captain Jones, my room-mate, in feeding ourselves. This was due to the known 'rackets' that were going on with the community feeding galley staff.

Officers imprisoned in Oflags sometimes had lower rank prisoners to serve as orderlies or batmen to them, although this sort of relationship tended to be very different to that observed between ranks during standard service life. Discipline and respect between the different levels of prisoner was ever-present but much relaxed compared to what it would have been like at home. Yet any form of crime was not to be tolerated within the community, as Eric Laker recalled in his Italian camp of PG70 at Monturano.

There has been an epidemic of thieving recently, parcels and bread chiefly have been missing. Bill Cummins told us that at 2am he had heard No 1 compound beating up a fellow who had been caught in the act. He told us he must have been getting a pretty rough handling because his screams were quite terrifying. Well I am afraid I have no sympathy for a thief under these circumstances.

As Tom Tateson described, from his perspective of Stalag IV-B, prisoner of war camps held men from many different backgrounds and in some cases this might mean that different nationalities would come into regular contact with one another.

Generally speaking, the Yanks were the ones who seemed to lose all self-respect. They seemed to make no attempt to keep themselves clean and tidy, and spent most of their time squatting in the dirt, playing cards. They gambled with cigarettes, some of which became so blackened and limp with so much handling that they would have been quite useless for smoking, but still retained their nominal value as currency. By contrast there were also some Sikh prisoners, permanent residents, who were always immaculately turned out, with clean uniforms, polished boots and knife-edge creases in their trousers. The contrast was not only in their appearance either. Although we had no contact with them other than seeing them walk about in their own compound, one large hut occupied by them had windows overlooking a path which we used. One day when I was walking along this path, a window opened and one of the Sikhs leaned out and handed me a whole torpedo shaped loaf. I was quite overcome and unable at first to believe I was being made a gift. However he made it plain that was the case, and blushing deeply in my confusion, I thanked him and walked on, quite bemused.

While the mix of nationalities and backgrounds within prisoner of war camps tended to vary, as did the camps themselves in both size and location, their basic layout and organisation tended to be common. Fairly remote places were usually chosen for the camps, which were surrounded by barbed wire, usually doubled and high enough to prevent easy scaling by the prisoners. Inside the wire fence it was common to have a single trip wire. If one ventured beyond this point the sentries would be liable to shoot. These sentries were chiefly of two kinds; those who would patrol outside the wire on a regular beat, while others were stationed in permanent sentry towers manning fixed machine guns to cover wide expanses of the camp.

Searchlights located on these towers would operate at night. The prisoner accommodation would usually be in wooden huts, laid out in rows with clear spaces set aside for the purpose of recreation.

There was usually some form of hospital building, as required by the provisions of the Geneva Conventions, for those prisoners who may require medical attention. The facility at Marlag-Milag was particularly impressive, boasting beds for 60 patients, an operating theatre, dental surgery, dispensary, massage room and kitchen. Doctors and surgeons resident in the camps would usually be kept very busy indeed, as prisoners would commonly use their captivity as an opportunity to resolve long-term ailments such as toothache, hernia or appendix troubles. One problem associated with recovering from medical issues was the poor diet experienced by those in captivity, however, which meant that any recuperation would take longer than might normally be the case.

Prisoners of war lacked privacy and were under constant surveillance, with their guards anxious to spot the tell-tale signs of an escape being planned. Sometimes the captors would go to the extent of hiding microphones in the walls of huts to overhear conversations, or position them to reveal sounds of digging. The Germans instigated what the prisoners termed 'ferrets' – guards who would wander throughout the prisoner enclosure, constantly peering through windows, eavesdropping, looking for signs of escape tunnels and checking on everyone and everything. The prisoners countered this by keeping their own watch on ferrets and the main gate, logging who came in and who exited. Some camps maintained incredibly detailed logs of how many guards were in the camp at any one time, since these would prove beneficial for the timing of any escape attempt. Guard dogs would often patrol around the compounds at night, while electric fences prevented barriers being scaled. Regular inspections, as described by 2nd Lieutenant Frank Stewart who was held in Oflag VII-B at Eichstatt, were designed to keep the prisoners on their toes.

All the signs are pointing to a search tomorrow. Searches are one of the banes of our lives. More than anything, I suppose, they outrage the Englishman's sense of property. At any moment a bevy of German soldiers may descend on your room and remove anything they don't think you ought to have. Not that I still have anything I oughtn't to have, but its singularly annoying having all one's possessions messed around with and turned upside down. In this camp they are fortunately more gentlemanly about it and the main objection is that we are kept out of our rooms for an indefinite period. If the whole camp is being searched at once this usually entails standing about on the parade ground for hours. Once we were kept out from 9am 'till 4.30pm, but usually the worst is over by lunch time.

One of the reasons that inspections were so disliked by the prisoners was that they disrupted their daily routine. Limitations on one's living space and activities meant that prisoners of war became creatures of habit, and anything unsettling that feeling of stability would cause major annoyance. Daily routine varied across camps but roughly followed the same pattern, with roll calls at the very beginning and end of each day and meals served at regular times, interspersed with opportunities for the prisoners to fill their time in whatever way they wished, whether it was sports activities, band practice, reading, writing, painting or just sleeping or chatting.

Morale varied across camps and localities but was heavily influenced by how the Allies were faring in the war, with expectations for liberation increasing as the conflict ploughed on and rising exponentially with each Allied victory. Communication with home was just as crucial, since an absence of letters or parcels could send even the most optimistic prisoner into spirals of despair, and we will look more closely at the importance of regular food in the following chapter. Yet in general terms, prisoners' spirits tended to be much higher than might be expected. Rarely was any belief expressed that the Allies would lose the war and that prisoners might become permanent inmates within a long-lasting Third Reich. It was rather the case that their time in enemy hands would be a temporary arrangement, albeit a highly inconvenient one. Their discomfort would simply have to be accepted until liberation. This positivity was arguably reliant on the common view among the Allies that the Axis powers, whether German or Italian, were 'in the wrong' and that their wartime successes so far would result only in failure in the long term. Anything that the Axis achieved or claimed should therefore be regarded as unjustified, unearned or just plain lies. This helped to generate a common feeling within the prisoner of war community that their resistance to authority was fully warranted. Many prisoners, but particularly officers, continued to believe that they were superior to their captors in both a moral and ethical way. By thinking in this manner the Allied prisoners were in effect subverting the normal relationship of captor and prisoner. Illustrative of this were Stanley Doughty and his comrades in PG52, who enjoyed devising ways to bait their Italian guards.

Many were the schemes thought up to annoy the sentries. We had time to think up these things and it was the only way in which you could restore any degree of self-respect. They were all old or handicapped guards, men who had little interest in the war and were only waiting, like us, for its end. The sentry boxes formed a cordon around the perimeter of the camp, and at night they used to call to one another, when instructed to do so by the Guard Commander in turn, I suppose to see if they were awake. Number one would call 'Allerta sentinella una' ['Awake sentry one'], then number two would sing like someone out of Italian opera, 'Allerta sentinella duo', and so on round the camp. You can imagine a whole campful of men, or more subtly only one prisoner, calling a number out of sequence. Funnily enough, although this infuriated them it was a month or more before the practice was stopped. Meanwhile chaos ensued.

This antagonistic attitude proved particularly helpful when it came to hindering the German attempts to recruit prisoners of war to join their war effort. The German Foreign Office and SS sought to raise a military unit known as the British Free Corps, made up from British prisoners of war, to assist in the fight against the Soviet Union on the Eastern Front. Initially, two 'holiday camps' were set up in June 1943 where prisoners could be sent to experience, for a short time, a much less restricted life and certain 'luxuries'. While placed in such a coercive environment, they would be exposed to propaganda to encourage them to join up against the Russians, portrayed by the Germans as the common foe. Eric Monckton, already full of hatred towards the Nazis for the ways in which they had treated him, expressed little tolerance for such ideas.

About the middle of March [1944], news came that the great 'Lord Haw-Haw' was to visit the camp and word was sent to the Nazi camp commander that if he put his nose into the camp no-one would be in the least responsible for his health. He never came into the camp but on March 27th he installed himself in the Nazi hut outside the main gate. He interviewed some dozen prisoners in this hut, the object evidently being propaganda and to get the prisoners' views for the formation of the British Free Corps, the pamphlet for which we passed round the camp later on. As Captain Jones and myself were near the main gate at the time, we were asked to go over and see him. All went well for the time being, and Joyce looked very fat and prosperous in his blue flannel pin-striped suit with a nice clean collar and pattern tie. He asked Captain Jones what his views on Russia were and the unprintable reply about himself and his parents, etc. were all that were necessary to find our two selves outside the hut and together in the gutter of the road.

A further recruitment drive followed later that year when leaflets were distributed within many camps, setting out the purpose of the British Free Corps and calling for support. Further visits from German recruiters attempted to encourage prisoners to join, although little success was achieved. Ultimately the British Free Corps scheme failed miserably, as membership peaked at only 27 men in January 1945. Some of these volunteers were apparently fooled into thinking that the organisation was sanctioned by the British government, and subsequently withdrew their offer of support. However the danger remained of Allied prisoners being exploited for propaganda purposes, as illustrated by an incident recalled by James Fulton, the British 'Man of Confidence' in Stalag XX-B.

One summer evening in 1944, Feldwebel *Myers, chief Stalag censor, arrived at Willenberg camp unexpectedly to interview me. On requesting the door of the bunk to be locked so that we would not be disturbed, I realised I would have to be on my mettle. He started by asking if I had read the article in the Camp magazine about the mass murder at Katyn Forest. I said I had but treated the publication as a propaganda sheet. He then asked if I would like a flight to Katyn, thereby proving whether it was the Germans or the Russians who had done the murders. Realising that there might be some trickery in it (perhaps photographed beside the mass grave then a caption added) I refused. Near the end of the interview a knock came at the door. I opened it and found one of my men who had come to report to me that an underofficer was going round the huts asking the prisoners if anyone wanted a flight to Katyn. I turned on Myers and told him in no uncertain manner what I thought of his dirty trick in holding me whilst his underling went round the prisoners. I pointed out clearly to him that he never stood a chance of anyone volunteering without them first coming to seek my advice. He left the camp disappointed, saying he was only carrying out orders.*

The relationship between prisoner and captor was dependent, perhaps more than anything else, on the attitude of the German or Italian guards and commandants towards the prisoners in their care. British prisoners in Italy considered themselves to be treated particularly unfairly, often feeling bullied. As a result, many ended up truly despising their captors. Broadly speaking, the Italian guards did indeed tend to be much harsher than their German counterparts. Examples of ill-treatment in both countries most commonly involved non-officer ranks, who were required to work and therefore had to suffer what was usually a poorer standard of living compared to commissioned prisoners. Stanley Doughty spent time as a prisoner in both Italian and German camps, and as such was well-placed to recognise how the German mentality differed from the Italian.

The German respect for law, order and authority was quite incredible – to British prisoners at least – and could always be relied upon from the Wehrmacht troops who were our guards. Like their Italian counterparts, they were elderly men or those with injuries which made them unsuitable for more active service. At this time too they could see the writing on the wall for Germany, and only wanted a quiet time and a quick end to the war. This treatment was not true of the prisoners of other nationalities, the Russians and Poles, who were in separate camps nearby and who were very poorly treated. We saw them from time to time, haggard, drawn and ragged, shambling their way along but there was no communication between us. We did experience the occasional search by Waffen SS troops who were in training in a nearby camp. They would come through our camp like the proverbial dose of salts looking for food hoarding for escape purposes or illegal radio sets, but always with a one-track mind and mentality. They never questioned how possessions, in full view, which could only be obtained from outside by barter, could be present in the camp. Presumably it was not in their orders. They were youngsters in their teens, blazing with arrogant Nazi zeal and superiority, into which they had been indoctrinated since their early years. Our old guards just lifted their eyes in mock horror and winked at us. Since it was they who had given us early warning of the search, the searchers found nothing.

Although life in Italian prisoner of war camps was largely similar to that experienced in Germany, the arrangements tended not to be as well-organised as those in German facilities. Camps in Italy were often hastily established by converting existing buildings, and any efforts to put non-commissioned prisoners to work were far from being as structured or intensive as those in German territory. After arriving on the Italian mainland following transport across the Mediterranean, Eric Laker entrained up the coast to Capua. Conditions for him and his fellow prisoners began to improve once they reached a transit camp where they started to be treated as 'official' prisoners of war.

We were put into these huts and things seemed a lot more rosy, one thick blanket and a palliase apiece, and that evening we received a Red Cross parcel between five. We were delighted and very excited to think that at last we had come under the protection of the Red Cross. After a time we received some of the clothing that most of us so badly needed. I got a light overcoat and a cap, the latter being most essential as we had all had our hair cropped off.

Then a week or so later, in December 1942, Eric was moved to the permanent camp of PG70 at Monturano, near the eastern coast of Italy.

This camp looked like a barracks with high buildings, a high wall, and a most impressive entrance. Inside were more large buildings like aeroplane hangars, and we were herded into the largest, the Central Hall, which was to be our 'home' until our compound buildings were finished. Here we were searched again, and I may remark at this point that in spite of the fact that this made the eighth time that

I had been searched since capture, I had managed all that time to keep my two watches concealed on me – a very good effort I think, although here and at Capua they were only searching for weapons.

At the rear of the buildings is a large open space of ploughed land, all inside the wall of course, with a wide path all round which makes a fairly decent means of exercise. I do not however get much time for exercise because two days after we arrived I got a permanent staff job in the compound post office, dreary and monotonous work, printing in quadruplicate on special forms, the name and address of each letter card and postcard and also the sender. However I get an extra piece of bread and cheese for the job so it is worth it. The loaf I split every evening with Tubby and we have it for supper, while we use our issue loaf half for breakfast and half for dinner. For food here we get 'coffee' at 7am, a watery skilly at noon and another at 4.30pm, a loaf and cheese about 5.30pm together with a sugar ration. On Thursday and Sunday we get no cheese but on Monday and Friday we get a microscopic piece of meat with the midday skilly. This magnificent menu however only lasted a short time, before very long we were down to one skilly a day, made from stinging nettles and other such weeds. Geoff Short was quite pleased one day to find a frog in his, one apparently that the Italians had missed! This Italian coffee is worth a mention here. Made very strong, it contains no sugar or milk, and is made actually not from coffee but ground acorns. We generally put sugar with ours (when we have any) and it makes a reasonable drink – hot at any rate.

The Italian Armistice was announced in September 1943, and by the end of the year some 50,000 prisoners of war who had been held captive in Italy were moved to new camps in Germany. In due course we shall look at how the British prisoners of war coped with this upheaval.

Life in the German prisoner of war camps changed as 1944 progressed. D-Day, 6 June 1944, saw the second front opening in western Europe; Rome and Paris were reclaimed by the Allies while the Eastern Front turned in the Soviet Union's favour. By the end of the year, German morale was therefore approaching its lowest ebb, and this affected the guards who would sometimes take their frustrations out on the prisoners under their care. Incidents of brutality by the Germans were recalled by Edgar Randolph, a Private in the 2/7th Field Ambulance of the Australian Imperial Force. He had been captured on Crete before ending up in Stalag VIII-B at Lamsdorf.

I saw a man under arrest who broke from his guard, raced down the road and turned into a compound – running along the double-barrack wall. The guard kneeled at the compound gate and fired, killing the prisoner. This was in the middle of the Stalag, with double-fenced compounds on each side of the one in question. No hope of escape – just close the compound and pick the man up. I also saw a prisoner who suddenly went berserk and, in full view of scores of men and many guards, ran across to a side gate of the camp and started to scale it. He was shot off the gate by the guard at a sentry box on the road, by a machine gunner in the machine gun tower not ten yards from the gate, and by a couple of guards outside the fence and not more than twenty to thirty yards away. All they had to do was wait until he got over and take him into custody – they preferred to shoot.

Sudden deaths of this nature were not unknown, as Tom Tateson recalled in the working camp at which he was based.

The reality of our position was revealed to us with a sickening shock when one day on returning from work we found the camp in a sombre atmosphere that was almost physically felt, and learned that one of the men on another working party had been shot dead by the civilian guard. The victim was an Australian who, by tragic coincidence, was celebrating his twenty-third birthday that day. It seemed that the civilian guard had seized one rather small and weak prisoner and was physically ill treating him. The Australian came to the assistance of his fellow prisoner and demanded that the German left him alone. For answer, the German drew a revolver and shot the Australian in the chest at point blank range. It took him about half an hour to die, during which time the German refused to let anyone come near him to try to render first aid, nor did he allow anyone to send for help. The German army officers in the camp took full statements from the witnesses and presumably some sort of enquiry was held, but I never heard of any result.

The twisted nature of Nazi ideology meant that for some ethnic groups, brutality was to be expected. Eric Laker witnessed two particular instances of cruelty that he never forgot.

A column of Jewesses was marched through the other day, no shoes or stockings but rags bound round their feet and legs, and they were being 'helped' along with whips and sticks. German culture! It reminded me of the time when I saw two German soldiers torturing a Russian slave worker on the road outside the mine. He was made to kneel down with a rough jagged piece of rock the size of a cricket ball under each knee, and hold a great lump of concrete with his arms stretched out in front of him. Every time he fell down or his arms fell he was beaten over the head with a rubber truncheon. Oh yes, they are nice people in this country.

It should be noted, however, that such extreme brutality was not experienced by all prisoners of war. Indeed, quite a few Allied prisoners actually enjoyed very good relations with their German captors. Prisoner Wilfred Sutton recalled one good-humoured guard who was popular among those held in Stalag IV-B at Mühlberg.

We in the RAF compound were in the care of an Unteroffizier named Schroeder. He was a typical German, tall, blonde and about 24 years old. He had a limp and it was thought that he had been wounded on the Russian front. He gave one the impression that he was a stickler for doing things the right way and according to the book but I know that underneath he had a great sense of humour. To illustrate this, we used to make all our cups, plates and in fact all our utensils from tins that were in the Red Cross parcels. We had rigged up a shelf on which these were stored and on one morning Schroeder decided that they were an untidy mess and swept them on to the floor with a swipe from his swagger stick. So we returned them to the shelf and nailed them in position, so you can imagine the expression on his face when next morning he tried to sweep them down again with his stick. You could see how it went up his arm and what he didn't call us in German was no-one's business. However, I was in the wash room when this incident took place and when he came into the room he just burst out laughing. On another occasion he gave two of the lads the job of tidying up the piles of sand we had outside the huts which were there in case we had a fire. They formed one mound to look like a grave, got two pieces of wood which they made into a cross on which they burnt the name 'Schroeder'. In front of everyone he just laughed. He just couldn't help himself.

Tom Tateson also reflected on the warm relations that sometimes existed with the Germans.

One of the guards, an Austrian built on the lines of Richard Tauber [a famous Austrian singer and actor] seemed keen to fraternize with us and tell us how homesick he was. One evening, after lock-up time, he came into the hut and sat showing us photographs of his wife and children, and getting positively maudlin; even tearful. He had, I think, been hitting the schnapps bottle pretty hard. We at last persuaded him that he had better leave before he got into trouble.

*He had been gone only a few minutes when someone called out,
'Christ, the silly old bugger's left his rifle behind.' We banged on
the door and shouted, and eventually another guard appeared. We
had to involve him, but did our best by a mixture of English, pidgin
German and hand signs to convey the message, 'Don't shop the poor
bastard – keep mum.'*

Relations between guards and prisoners were particularly strained
during instances of reprisals. There were several examples of reprisal
actions in German camps over the course of the war, carried out in
direct response to perceived faults by the Allies. Perhaps the most
widespread was that which followed the Dieppe Raid of August
1942, when it was alleged that German prisoners had been tied
up, blindfolded or shackled. Similarly, following a raid on the
Channel Island of Sark in October 1942, some Germans were later
discovered to have been shot dead whilst shackled. In response to
these perceived atrocities, some 3,000 Allied prisoners of war held
mainly at Oflag VII-B, Stalag VIII-B and Stalag 383 were put into
shackles for a number of weeks. Lieutenant Harwood was one of
the British officers held captive in Oflag VII-B at Eichstatt, and
recalled the announcement of this harsh measure.

*On this particular morning we were on parade waiting to be counted
when we noticed that the sentry-boxes round the camp had their
flaps down and the guards, who had been doubled, were manning
their automatics. These guns, needless to say, were all trained on
us. The* Kommandant, *a man of the worst type, strutted onto the
field and told the SBO to produce 120 officers to be manacled. He
hastened to add that should we give any trouble the sentries had
received orders to fire on us immediately. I found out later that the
Germans also had mortars placed outside the camp which they
contemplated using should we resist the order. The SBO called up
his company commanders, explained the situation, and instructed*

them to produce a certain number of officers from each company. Those detached were then marched off the parade ground to collect their bedding... I feel sure the lack of fuss and bother, which was a sign of excellent discipline, disappointed the Kommandant *who was longing for an excuse for a spot of illicit shooting.*

The Germans arrived first thing each morning to manacle the officers and then again at night to release them for sleep. However, these fellows who had the misfortune to be handcuffed soon found out that it was comparatively easy to free themselves with the aid of an old nail and a boot used as a hammer. They would sit in their new quarters playing cards or reading with their manacles close at hand which could be slipped on at the approach of any German. In the mornings they paraded in their greatcoats, correctly manacled, and during the day Germans would make periodical inspections to make sure that no attempts had been made to get free. The fact that the officers had by now discarded their greatcoats and yet were still manacled never impressed itself on the German mentality. Although no one pretended to take this business seriously it was noticed after a month or so that the manacles were having a bad effect on the nerves. Accordingly a roster was compiled from volunteers who were prepared to relieve their friends. The Germans did not seem to mind provided they could report to the Wehrmacht *that the correct number of British officers were undergoing this highly civilised treatment.*

Other, smaller reprisal actions might involve the confiscation of personal items from prisoners, including towels, razors and utensils. Such a policy was carried out in September 1942 in response to the alleged confiscation of the personal possessions of German officers captured in North Africa. As with most reprisals, the strategy simply petered out over time. In a rather characteristic act of turning the situation to their own amusement, the British prisoners responded to the lack of razors by challenging each other to grow the longest beard. Eric Laker, held captive in Italy, remembered how more minor reprisal punishments were instigated by his captors. On this occasion, it was as punishment in response to the prisoners burning wood for their stoves.

10 March 1943. Horrible news today. Because of the damage done to beds, pegs, etc. being taken for brews, all tea, cocoa and coffee is being taken from parcels and two brews a day being issued from the cookhouse. This is a big blow, and the Italians are going further and are stopping all brewing and cooking. This makes porridge and such things as Yorkshire pudding mixture absolutely useless. Oh and to crown it all we are getting half pay for four weeks to pay for the damage. That does not worry me in the slightest but the brewing business is a knockout blow. Life was hard enough without having to suffer for some thoughtless destructive idiots. I only hope this ban will be lifted after a time.

The ultimate reprisal undertaken by the German authorities was arguably the execution of 50 Allied officers by the Gestapo. This occurred shortly after the 'Great Escape' from Stalag Luft III on 25 March 1944, and was intended to act as a clear warning against similar such breakouts. We will look at this event in more detail in a subsequent chapter.

Most prisoners of war suffered from psychological problems as a result of their incarceration. Forgetfulness and confusion were common traits among prisoners with limited means to keep their brains mentally stimulated. Lieutenant Harwood of the 5th Battalion, East Kent Regiment had been among the first large batch of prisoners captured during the Battle of France in May 1940.

I discovered that it was getting harder and harder to concentrate on anything. I think the real reason for this malady, because it really was a malady, was that most of us lived in a sort of day-dream, trying subconsciously to make our minds a blank and so blot out the present.

Malnutrition helped to accentuate this state. I would read a book one day and probably forget not only the title, the name of the author, but also the contents by the following day. I witnessed an incident which amply illustrates what I mean. Four officers were playing bridge in the recreation room, a large, high-ceilinged hall with a balcony running along one end, used on Sundays for church services. One of the officers, being dummy, announced that he intended to go and relieve himself while his partner played the hand. The hand was completed and the fellow did not return. The other three waited for about a quarter of an hour and then went to the lavatory to see what had happened. No sign of the missing officer. Feeling rather annoyed, they went up to the balcony where bridge was also in progress, looking for someone else to take the place of the missing man. Much to their amazement, sitting at a table calmly playing bridge was their original fourth who looked up, smiled vaguely and went on playing. When it was pointed out to him in no uncertain manner that he was already in another game, he dropped his cards, apologised profusely to the other three with a blank expression, and said he had completely forgotten.

It was also not uncommon for prisoners to experience regular bouts of depression – commonly known as 'barbed wire fever' – which proved contagious and spread within the confines of the camp. Feelings of melancholy or despair were perhaps inevitable when so many bodies were living close together under such difficult circumstances, as Eric Monckton recorded.

Some of the prisoners just fell into a state of apathy, only taking interest in their bunks, feeding time, and lazing around doing nothing. For these, it was a good thing that there were the three musters every day in the summer and two per day in the winter, from which one had to be in the hospital or have a special permit to be absent, unless working outside the camp.

Specific symptoms such as lethargy, fits of sudden anger, and memory loss were much more commonly experienced by officers and senior NCOs; other rank prisoners based in working camps were largely kept busy and perhaps had less time to become introspective or be overly troubled by the lack of private space. Things like lethargy could also be blamed upon the poor diet, as Eric Laker observed.

All day today I have been feeling fed up, miserable and very home sick. I suppose it is natural that under these circumstances one gets such fits of depression, and the fact that no-one seems to know when the parcels can be expected does not help. There are even no rumours floating about which I think points to the fact that nearly everybody is feeling the same. There has not been an issue of letter cards or postcards for over two weeks now, simply because the Eyeties have none. This of course means that at home they will not hear and they will worry over that. Oh dear what a life!

The support network within the prisoner community was usually strong, with each man looking out for their own, and as a result severe depression and suicides were quite rare, counting for only 22 British prisoner deaths throughout the war – a very tiny proportion. However, formal diagnosis of mental illness was also very uncommon, perhaps because it was one of the criteria for medical repatriation. Some prisoners chose to exploit this and medical officers were therefore perhaps overly strict in choosing not to recognise mental issues. It should also be said that some deaths were not reported as suicides when perhaps they should have been. As Stanley Doughty observed, 'Quite a few died by merely deciding to do so, especially in the bitter cold of the mid-European winter.' It was also the case that attempted suicide was not necessarily reported, like in a specific case recalled by Corporal Harvey, held captive in Stalag VIII-B at Brzeg.

The three-tier bunks were situated to one side of the barrack, leaving an open space where we had tables for eating our food or recreation. It was midday and we were all gathered around waiting for the rations to come, when we noticed a middle aged South African man and he appeared to be ill with his blanket pulled up to his chin. We decided to check and when we turned the blanket back he was covered in blood. He had a razor blade and he had slashed his forearms. We got one of the table tops and pulled him and his bedding straight on it and four of us jog-trotted down the road to the main gate to get him into hospital. I think they saved him but I never saw him again so they may have kept him in for observation. Again, a case of severe depression and I'm thankful I never got in that state. I couldn't forget Edith and the children waiting for me to come home and look after them and this gave me the strength to survive.

But the large number of men living in close proximity to each other, sharing facilities and with little opportunity for privacy, led to a difficult situation. Sometimes the closeness of prisoners could easily lead to disagreements, as was the case with Corporal Harvey.

Everyone was now stretched as tight as a bowstring and very touchy. I had one friend, who when we were first captured suggested we should stick together until it was all over. It sounded alright and we kept together until one afternoon the subject turned to food (as always) and we were talking of our favourite food. His dreams were all on roast beef, Yorkshire pudding and lashings of vegetables and my thoughts were for a freshly baked brown loaf and a large chunk of cheese. Sounds harmless enough now, but somewhere along the line we got into a fierce argument and that finished our beautiful friendship. Following this experience I vowed never again to enter into any close relationship with anyone.

It was really down to the prisoners themselves to find ways of brightening up their dull existence by whatever means they could. Prisoner of war camps were bland, unfriendly locations at the best of times and so efforts were made to bring a degree of homeliness to the place. The interior of huts, where the prisoners spent much of their time, could be adapted and decorated in order to bring a taste of home.

Some prisoners, such as Eric Laker, tried to lift their own morale by putting a positive spin on their current situation. Establishing the appropriate mental attitude to captivity was all important.

I have been thinking recently of some of the advantages of being a POW. I came to the conclusion that even under these very trying circumstances there must be some advantages over the fellow still in the army. We for instance, while under a certain amount of discipline, are not subject to pukka army discipline. We do not have to worry, as we did in the desert, about moves being ordered at perhaps two hours' notice. The sudden rush and flurry of having to pack up at once, never knowing what we were going to, all that is past now, thank goodness. And lastly, but by no means least, is the important safety factor. No longer do we run the risk of 'snuffing it' by means of a Stuka or one of those beastly mortar bombs. The risk that was always in my mind, no matter how free from care I appeared on the surface, of ending up maimed, minus a limb or worse still my sight, no longer exists. With reasonable luck, provided I can keep fit, I should return home more or less as I left.

Christmas was always a time for the prisoners to try to make best of a bad situation, as Tom Tateson remembered. Everybody made the extra effort to contribute to the jovial and festive holiday, putting aside their hardships as best they could and combining resources to prepare for the big day.

We had been preparing for this day, which was allowed as an extra day off work, for some time. Someone in our hut constructed a most convincing and effective dart board out of coiled strips of cardboard from Red Cross parcel boxes, and wire from God knows where. The darts must have been bought from the Germans by barter. We also managed to buy in a keg of something said to be beer. It was very weak stuff, but added greatly to the festive atmosphere. It was a crisp, bright sunny day, with a thin layer of fresh snow, and the atmosphere was exhilarating. Everyone's spirits leapt up, and an air of cheerful affability prevailed. Perhaps without realizing it we had sunk to a pretty low level of apathy, and the combination of the arrival of the day of celebration we had prepared for, and the brilliant weather, induced an atmosphere of bonhomie that was both very pleasant and almost startling. Christmas greetings were exchanged enthusiastically between complete strangers.

Each hut had made its own preparations for the day, and the extent of these depended on the individual group's degree of access to German sources of barter. The privileged hut, that occupied by the camp leader and his cronies had, incredibly, managed to procure a turkey. They had this cooking nicely on their stove when two of the German guards burst in, and yelling abuse at the high spirited men, hurled the bird off the stove and onto the floor. At the time I felt this to be a deed most foul, particularly considering for how long the men had been saving up cigarettes and Red Cross food to trade for this special luxury. I even referred to it in my diary as a Nazi 'atrocity'. With hindsight, knowing that the German civilians were by now on very short rations, I completely understand the rage of the guards to see prisoners indulging themselves so, no matter that it was their own people who had provided the turkey.

Morale was also determined by levels of hygiene, a factor of great importance in prisoner of war camps where many bodies were living in close proximity to each other with limited access to showering. As

Stanley Doughty recalled, the true bugbear of the prisoner community was lice, which commonly affected all to differing degrees.

Washing in cold water in the summer time might have been one thing, but in the winter only a few hardy souls could face up to it, and lice and bed-bugs were a fact of life. With lice of course comes the fear of typhus so regular delousing sessions were held nightly in all the huts, but the bugs won of course, as they always will. They can be 'popped' between one's nails or with a lighted cigarette end if one is squeamish. They did provide pellets to be fired over the wire on the guards at night though, with the aid of catapults made from braces, which provided amusement if nothing else.

As a consequence of these infestations, delousing was a regular activity among the prisoners. Eric Laker stressed the importance of keeping clean as a prisoner of war and not letting one's standards slip.

I went through my usual delousing process at dinnertime and caught the usual score or so. The thought of this vermin is positively revolting and at times makes me feel really bad. My skin, as is everyone's, is literally smothered, yes smothered with bites, which directly I start to rub them come up in a bright red inflamed patch. Roll on the day when I can burn my clothes and have a hot bath. I often thank my lucky stars that I always kept myself fit, and no doubt being young helps me to take it better, the sparse food, lack of exercise and the lice. Some of the fellows have let themselves go completely and take no care of themselves at all. Some are almost walking skeletons but of course that is not their fault. My God when is all this going to end. Sometimes I want to scream and shout; sometimes I want to cry and have great difficulty in making myself believe it will end – must end somewhen, and that way, way ahead, lies something better, something that is worth waiting for. Sometimes it is very hard though. Three months now and it seems like thirty years. What a hideous waste it all is.

Hopes of any improvement to living conditions in prisoner of war camps were pinned on the findings of camp inspectors. Occasional inspections of camps were undertaken by representatives from the International Committee of the Red Cross, yet evidence suggests that relatively little changed as a consequence of their findings. Such visits, however, remained a welcome event among the prisoners who appreciated the reminder that the German and Italian authorities were reliant on observing the Geneva Conventions, to whatever degree they really did follow the agreed international standards for treating prisoners of war. However, quality of life as a prisoner was largely governed by one thing more than any other. If we had to identify the most significant aspect of prisoner of war life which was shared by all men, whatever their background and whichever camp they happened to be held in, it would be food. In order to maintain anything approaching a healthy diet, prisoners really had to rely on the contents of parcels in order to supplement the basic rations given to them by their captors.

3 | Food, Parcels and Letters

Without the British Red Cross parcels, the health of all in the camp would have suffered

The availability of food was without question the most important consideration for any prisoner of war. With little else to occupy their minds, thoughts of the next meal tended to dominate all others. Since the sort of nutritious and enjoyable 'comfort food' associated with home was clearly unobtainable in captivity, the poor alternative for prisoners was to do the best they could with the limited rations available. While the authorities in both Germany and Italy issued set prison rations, these largely failed to provide the adequate nutrition that hungry prisoners required. Those in captivity therefore had to depend on the greater variety supplied by the regular food parcels provided by the Red Cross. For this reason, the delivery of a Red Cross parcel became an exciting occasion, and the contents helped to improve all prisoners' quality of life throughout the war to a massive degree. Food was always foremost in prisoners' minds and, as Tom Tateson recalled, pretty much every conversation always returned to the same subject.

The constant topics of conversation were food and the prospects of the war ending, but mainly food. Sex was well down the list, in fact the only time our thoughts and conversation turned in that direction was after a delivery of Red Cross parcels, when we had indulged in a good meal. The subject of food never palled, and we would concoct fantasy menus including such things as steak and kidney pudding, jam roly-poly and custard. Top of the list of favourites to salivate about though was bacon and egg, usually with the embellishment of 'and lots of dip running down your chin'.

Such a notion was reinforced by Wilfred Sutton, who noted a remarkable change in conversations once regular supplies of Red Cross parcels began to arrive in his camp.

Prior to this one could walk through the hut and at every bed one could hear about the super meals the lads had eaten before the war. Juicy fillet steaks with bags of mushrooms and fried potatoes, wonderful sweets with lashings of cream, crisp duck with orange sauce washed down the claret and so on, but as soon as the inner man was full of food the same men would be talking not of the food but of the legs of the waitress or the bust dimensions of some girl they had dated. It proved one point of course. Self-preservation was a stronger instinct than sex.

Prisoners of war were forever indebted to the source of such food parcels. What became known as the International Committee of the Red Cross (ICRC) had been established in Geneva in 1863, with its initial aim being to provide neutral and impartial help to relieve suffering in times of war. The Committee were instrumental in drafting the first Geneva Convention of 1864, which recognised the status of medical services on the battlefield and set out standards for the treatment of wounded soldiers. In time, a number of national societies sprung up across the world which were affiliated to the main ICRC, but with each responsible for vulnerable individuals from their own nations. The British National Society for Aid to the Sick and Wounded in War was formed in 1870 and would be formally renamed as the British Red Cross Society in 1905. Upon the outbreak of the Second World War in September 1939, the British Red Cross coordinated their activities with the Order of St John of Jerusalem, as they had done during the First World War, and became known as the Joint War Organisation. It was this name that was often stamped on the cardboard boxes which were hurriedly opened by hungry prisoners.

One of the most valuable services provided by the Red Cross was their Wounded, Missing and Relatives Department which helped people back home to search for information concerning servicemen who were reported as missing or wounded in action. Servicemen declared missing might sometimes turn up in military hospitals or, far more often, as prisoners of war. Once a prisoner of war was officially registered with the Red Cross, their details were passed to the British authorities who would in turn notify the family. However the inevitable delays in this process meant an agonising wait, sometimes for several months, with a fair number of 'missing' troops being presumed dead in the meantime by their loved ones.

Tom Tateson, newly captured during the Battle for Normandy, had arrived at his first permanent camp of Stalag XII-A at Limburg.

It was about this time that we were for the first time registered by the Red Cross. This was a considerable boost to our morale, as we had always felt that until this was done we could be disposed of without trace and without undue hesitation. We were also issued with printed postcards to address to our next-of-kin to let them know that we were prisoners of war. No message was permitted other than the deletion as appropriate of the words 'I am well' or 'I am wounded'. The essential thing was though that Olive should know that I was alive, and it was a great relief to be able to send this message. As it turned out, that relief was unwarranted, since it was many months before the card reached her.

While communication with home was crucial for the prisoners, it tended to be the parcels received from the Red Cross which were of greatest immediate importance. The Joint War Organisation's Prisoners of War Department was responsible for packing and dispatching parcels to British prisoners of war across the world. Packed in Britain, the parcels were then sent to locations in Italy and Germany via the ICRC based in neutral Switzerland. Similar food parcels were also provided by other country's Red Cross organisations and it was not uncommon for these to be distributed to Allied prisoners of war regardless of their nationality, so British prisoners might sometimes receive Canadian or American parcels. Over 20 million food parcels were sent to British prisoners of war throughout the conflict, reaching a peak of five and a half million in 1942. This large-scale charitable work was largely funded by generous donations from ordinary people. Indeed, by the end of the war, the British Red Cross could reveal that they had spent £52 million without incurring any debt. Tom Tateson was now fully registered and eligible for parcels.

Oddly enough, I cannot remember at what stage we started to receive Red Cross parcels. Individual items in them acquired specific values in terms of cigarettes, and trading was common. It has never ceased to astonish me that anyone on a semi-starvation diet would trade food for cigarettes, but of course it is a well-known phenomenon. Apart from this example of what seemed to me lack of will power, there were also many men who were incapable of rationing themselves to make their food spin out. The most bizarre example of this was a Yank who acquired a bowl from somewhere and emptied into it the contents of every tin and packet from his Red Cross parcel – Spam, dried milk, condensed milk, chocolate, Yorkshire pudding mix, etc., etc. – even tea. He then stirred it all up together and set about eating the lot. Needless to say he subsequently vomited the lot.

Each parcel would contain as many as 11 tins of various shapes and sizes, containing things like biscuits, vegetables, margarine, dried egg, condensed milk, processed cheese, meat roll or sardines. Several variants of food parcel existed, but all would include the basic staples of chocolate, tea and sugar. Sometimes sweets might be included, or even pancake batter. The early parcels also included cigarettes or tobacco, but these eventually came to be separated from food and sent in separate packages, probably due to their bulk. Considerable thought went into the packing of each parcel, with all varieties of prisoner being considered. Special food parcels were designed for men in sick quarters and consisted mainly of high-concentrate liquid foods such as Bovril, Horlicks and Ovaltine. Parcels intended for Indian prisoners might have curry powder and rice, for instance, instead of the usual Anglo-centric contents. Scottish Red Cross parcels would contain rolled oats. Whatever the contents, this extra food would be added to the standard rations doled out to each prisoner which, as Eric Monckton recalled, were largely inadequate.

The food provided by the Nazis consisted mainly of potatoes, black bread, ersatz butter, and occasionally a little meat, oatmeal and barley. A tasteless jam and cheese ration was issued every week. These rations were very meagre and if the Nazi civilian population received no more than we did and of such a poor substitute nature, they must have certainly been in a starving condition and unfit for any great amount of work. Without the British Red Cross parcels, the health of all in the camp would have suffered and there would have been many more illnesses than there were.

Towards the end of the war, when rations were even lower quality and smaller in size due to shortages, the existence of Red Cross food parcels proved particularly important. It was sometimes even the case that the prisoners were receiving a better, more varied diet than their guards – which might lead to the Germans distributing the contents of food parcels in a less democratic way, keeping certain contents for themselves.

Stanley Doughty, held captive in the Italian camp PG52, recalled the excitement of the first Red Cross parcels arriving.

One day, after countless rumours, a distribution of Red Cross parcels was made. I can't remember just what fraction of a parcel each was the distribution, it varied greatly over the time between none, a whole one each, and one between 12 – an impossible situation. Usually 'syndicates' of friends were formed to cope with this division, each syndicate changing in number to meet the split required, but always with the one unlucky enough to be selected by lot to be the divider, the last to get his share. Much thought went into the relative values of an Oxo cube and a spoonful of powdered milk in order to distribute the parcels fairly. Some of the meals which the syndicates cooked were quite unusual, one might almost say weird. Sweet and savouries went together, and in order that as fair a distribution as possible be made, almost everything turned out as a stew.

Usually, the contents of food parcels would be distributed throughout the camp and shared equally through communal dining. Some prisoners favoured preparing their own food, though, or might more commonly share the task with others in their particular room or hut. Either way, the contents of parcels were a godsend to those in captivity who would otherwise have struggled to subsist on the basic official camp rations. Eric Monckton stressed their importance to maintaining a healthy diet.

All were very thankful that the Germans allowed the Red Cross parcels into the camp as without them there would have been extreme illness throughout the camp from the meagre and rotten

German supply of food. My partner and myself did much better on our own than we had faced with the community feeding, both in variety, quality and in quantity. Being able to decide and make arrangements between ourselves as to what we would have the following day, within the limits of our Red Cross parcels, gave us a greater satisfaction than the routine order of community feeding. We also had the advantage of preparing dishes with eggs, onions, flour, etc. which we had bought with various commodities in our parcel, which was vastly better than when community feeding, and we felt much better in health for our food partnership.

Sometimes, as demonstrated by Tom Tateson, the contents of parcels could be adapted inventively in order to make the most out of whatever food resource was available.

Another very valuable item in the parcels was a packet of sultanas. These I used to make a sandwich with two slices of my bread ration and took this with me to work, wrapped in an old field dressing. Usually at break time there would be a fire, round which we gathered, and I would fry my sandwich on a shovel held over the fire. The dirt didn't matter, and the sultanas swelling in the sandwich produced a very satisfying and tasty snack.

The key to sharing food was to ensure its equal distribution, and prisoners attached enormous importance to the notion of each man receiving his correct allotted share. Food arrangements in the temporary transit camp at Bari were even more difficult, as Corporal Harvey recalled, as this was before the prisoners had been registered with the Red Cross and could receive additional food parcels.

In the absence of parcels, everything connected with our daily rations had to be scrupulously fair and way above any suspicion. As a Corporal in our tent I was asked to undertake the doling out of the soup for our 20 men. *The Dixie was collected from the cookhouse, at the appropriate time, by two men, one from our tent and one from the tent opposite and placed squarely between our two tents for everyone to see. We had already agreed to line up in rotation and move up one each day, with the first of that day dropping back to the end next day. This was necessary because the soup was mainly vegetable, sometimes thickened with macaroni and naturally the bottom of the Dixie would be thickest, although we stirred at regular intervals. Some days it was all thick so the rotation idea was still satisfactory. My own tin was carried by the man who slept next to me so that ensured I took my turn in the rotation. So I stood at one end of the Dixie with the serving tin at the ready, opposite the man from the other tent. Both serving tins were identical, with a mark to show we both served the same to each man. In the event of any soup being left in the Dixie, after the issue to each man, we had a separate roster.*

The bread ration was also another vexing problem and continued all the time we were in Italy. Finally it was agreed that as rations were always issued for 20 men, 2 men in rotation would take a blanket to collect the bread ration, i.e. 20 small bread cakes (which could differ slightly in shape and size). To save any further dissension, the corners of the blanket were drawn up to form a bag and each of the 20 men, in rotating turn, was allowed to put his arm into the bag, without seeing the bread, and pull out the first loaf he touched. Woe betide any man caught fishing around for the biggest one. Any unfairness usually finished up with a fight. To the reader this may seem ridiculous and foolish but at the time it was happening it was very real and a serious business.

Tom Tateson, ultimately posted to a labour camp at Bitterfeld, understandably placed huge importance on rations at a time when he and his fellow prisoners required every calorie they could obtain in order to ensure that they had enough energy for work. The extent to which Tateson and his comrades went in order to ensure fair distribution of the daily ration was, with hindsight, quite incredible.

Each room had its own leader, who had the onerous task of distributing the rations fairly among 20 half-starved men. I was elected to this post and managed to devise a system which could be seen to be fair. With the bread, if for example we were on a ration of one loaf between three, one of the three would be given the loaf to cut up. The other two took it in turns to have first pick and the 'carver' had the remaining piece. This encouraged him to be scrupulously exact in his division of the loaf. In the case of meat, I would arrange 20 portions on the table in front of me. Each man was given an 'individual' number which he retained. I then had one man at the back of the room turn round so that he could not see the table, and as I indicated one portion at random I would ask him to call out any number from one to twenty. That numbered man then collected that portion and the others followed in sequence along the row of portions. The division of the block of margarine never seemed to carry the same degree of tension, so I simply cut it up and it was lucky dip.

Christmas was a time for celebration, and the centrepiece for such an important holiday always involved enjoying special food wherever possible. Eric Laker recalled how Christmas was celebrated in 1942 in his camp in Italy.

On the Sunday before, that was the 20th, a carol service was held to which Tubby, Alan and myself went. I heartily enjoyed singing the usual carols, and it brought back many memories of happier Christmases of the past. For sermon the padre read an abridged version of the story of the 'Fourth Wise Man', a novel and enjoyable brain wave. For Christmas Day we had all been promised a special Red Cross Christmas parcel containing pudding, cake, chocolate biscuits, sweets, chocolate, braised steak and macaroni, and they did not arrive, so every man had his next issue parcel brought forward, every one receiving a Canadian parcel on Christmas Eve. The Canadian parcels were standard and contain luncheon meat, corned beef, salmon, sardines, cheese, chocolate, ¼ lb tea, ¼ lb sugar, a large tin of Klim (powdered milk), 1 lb tin of jam or marmalade (if jam, you get coffee instead of tea) and best of all 1 lb of genuine butter. In the English parcels you get ½ lb margarine and the other contents vary.

Here I will describe our menu on Christmas Day. We had hot water issued in the morning instead of the usual coffee, so we made tea and had two of the marvellous Canadian biscuits. Directly after tea we went to Holy Communion and directly after that outside for the only roll call of the day (usually there are two). After roll call we adjourned to the brewing-up patch and prepared breakfast, which consisted of fried onions and a whole tin of steak and mixed vegetables, left over from our previous parcel, which we heated up and had with our half loaf and two biscuits apiece. At midday we had the one skilly of the day, double rations and double thick. Quite good and tasty. After dinner we made another brew which we had with another biscuit, followed by chocolate. For tea, about 4pm, we had more tea, a tin of salmon between us, stewed prunes and cream. It tasted wonderful.

New Year celebrations brought further excitement, as their meal on 2 January 1943 contained a novel surprise.

For the first time since being captured we had a taste (an exceedingly small one) of potatoes in the skilly at noon. The issue worked out at approximately 1 lb to every eight men, so some were lucky and got a complete spud while others, like myself, got perhaps a piece of peel and a piece perhaps the size of a finger nail. Still it did remind one of what potatoes tasted like once. I wish we received more potatoes; it seems absurd that an agricultural country like Italy should be short, but what happens is that Germany takes them all, or a very large proportion.

Finally, 11 days later than originally planned but still hugely appreciated, the Red Cross parcels intended for Christmas arrived on 5 January 1943.

A load of Christmas parcels came in today and we were issued with one between two. Had a good day. The parcel came up about 11am and we at once had the chocolate and a few sweets. For supper we had a loaf apiece and then the pudding between us. The contents of the Christmas parcel were Christmas cake (Huntley and Palmers), ½ lb chocolate biscuits (Peak Freans), Christmas pudding (Mortons), tin braised steak and macaroni, tin steak and tomato pudding, tin Meltis confectionary, ¼ lb chocolate, ½ lb butter, and the usual cheese, tea, sugar, milk and soap. A parcel designed for one day, but one person would have a job to kill it in one day – some tried at Christmas and suffered!

Apart from their nutritional benefit, another reason for the popularity of Red Cross parcels was the box itself. The packaging of thick cardboard, or plywood in the case of Canadian parcels, could be utilised for all sorts of different purposes. Boxes proved perfect for improvised bedside tables, book shelves, and even for lining escape tunnels. Proper timber was usually very difficult to get hold of. The string tied around each parcel could be reutilised in order to make rope, while empty food tins represented the only readily available source of metal in many camps and were therefore used for a variety of purposes: as cups or mugs, utensils, flower pots, candle holders or even makeshift stoves. Frank Stewart recalled the facilities which existed in Oflag VII-B for making the most out of these odd bits and pieces.

I've never been into the carpenter's shop but I know that their continual trouble is lack of material. For this they have to rely, I think completely, on the wooden crates in which Canadian Red Cross parcels and bulk food from the Argentines come, and most of this is only 3-ply wood. But they run a more vigorous line in tannery, if that's the right word. Tins are collected after use and bashed into shape and it is amazing what useful articles have been produced such as cooking stoves, pots and dishes for the oven. This craft has certainly been developed tremendously. British Red Cross boxes are, as you know, made of cardboard and therefore not much use to the carpenters but they turn out a very good line in brushes made from the string.

One of the problems which prisoners had to address was how to keep hold of the empty boxes, since in some camps this was far from straightforward. But the necessity of finding suitable fuel for heat and cooking was a strong incentive for theft. Stanley Doughty was held in PG52 at Chiavari.

The cardboard boxes the Red Cross parcels came in were very useful, but the Italians wanted them as raw material for the war effort so they could only be obtained by stealing. On parcel distribution days the syndicates would walk over in turn, as a body, to the distribution hall, and one elected member of it would go up to collect a parcel. It was opened in front of him, every tin being stabbed with a bayonet to prevent saving them for escape attempts, and the string and outer cardboard being put into two separate piles. It was the duty of other prisoners, under escort, to take blanket loads of this material through the gate into the Italian compound. Many were the devious ways in which load after load was spirited away for our use. Whether the Italians knew and shut their eyes to this, or whether we were really defeating them we never knew, but we got our fuel together with a nice warm feeling that we had outwitted the opposition.

The contents of food parcels could also prove valuable as commodities to exchange for other materials. Tobacco and real coffee (as opposed to the German or Italian ersatz variety issued as part of the standard ration) were particularly valued in this regard. The corruptibility of German or Italian guards was the definite weak link in the captors' security, although any bribery had to be undertaken in a careful fashion. First, small insignificant favours were requested in exchange for perhaps a few cigarettes, before the bribery increased in more serious ways. Before the guard realised what was happening, he was caught in the net and implicated so far that he would have to continue with the arrangement, fearful of his superiors finding out and the inevitable punishment which would follow. It was not unknown for some guards to accept significant bribes in return for items such as clothes, tools, maps or even identity passes – all of which were largely obtained by the prisoners with a view to escaping.

While food parcels were the Red Cross' main humanitarian concern, they also packaged and sent parcels for other purposes. Some parcels aimed to maintain the prisoners' morale and mental health, with such packages including educational materials such as books. There were also medical parcels with items such as spectacles or false teeth, and recreational ones with sporting equipment or musical instruments. The ICRC also acted as courier for parcels packed by prisoners' families and next-of-kin, with registered individuals able to send private parcels to prisoners on a quarterly basis. Severe restrictions existed on what could be sent in order to meet the criteria of not assisting the war effort. Any clothing could only be of certain colours, for instance, while all printed material required checking by the censor.

Letters too were exchanged via the Red Cross and, as their only tangible link with home, prisoners attached huge importance to the receipt of both letters and parcels. Many men, such as Tom Tateson, had a wife or children waiting for them back home, so their extended period of separation might only be alleviated by personal messages of wellbeing. Before receiving notification that her husband was a prisoner of war, Olive Tateson had spent five months worrying about his uncertain fate.

> *Periods of relaxation and comparative happiness were however marred by worry about Olive, and guilt that I was living fairly comfortably whilst she must be worried sick and facing the birth of our second child not knowing whether I was alive or dead. It would have been impossible for anyone at Battalion HQ to have known who had survived that night of the 18th June. In fact I learned from Olive when I eventually returned to England that she first received a telegram to say that I was missing, and shortly after that a personal letter of condolence from Lt Wilson, the Signals Officer, saying that 'the last time he was seen, he was in the thick of the battle,' a kind letter, but ominous in its implications. Immediately after we had been registered by the Red Cross, we had been issued with the printed postcards for us to address to our next-of-kin. My card did not reach Olive until the week before Robert was born on 15th October. The mental agony she must have endured during this long period from May, when she had last heard from me, must have been terrible and probably contributed to the anxiety which troubled her for the rest of her life.*

Each prisoner was allowed to send a certain number of letters and postcards which, for most of those held captive in Europe, usually meant two letters and four postcards every month. Letter forms were provided to prisoners with 26 lines to fill with text, or postcards with 7 lines. All written text was subject to censorship by the Italians or Germans, which meant that most messages sent home had to be largely bland and nondescript in nature. The speed of mail exchange varied, but generally a letter took about five weeks to pass in either direction, meaning that an exchange of correspondence might take several months. The first bulk batch of prisoner of war mail to arrive from Germany was on 27 August 1940, which consisted of 30 bags containing about 120,000 letters and cards. Tom Tateson had to wait some eight months before hearing from his wife.

Some post had now got through to the camp but I had to endure a number of disappointments before I received my first letter from Olive sometime in February [1945]. This letter was out of sequence, and references to 'Bobby' were the first clue I had that I had a second son. Although I later received earlier letters, some never reached me. One item of mail which did reach me was a Christmas card from my employers, one of the major composite insurance companies. On it they wished themselves prosperity in the coming year. A delightful example of insensitivity.

In addition to the time delay affecting the exchange of mail, regular correspondence was difficult because it was not uncommon for letters to be lost en route or arrive in the wrong chronological order. This often made long distance relationships very difficult to maintain, particularly in the case where young unmarried men attempted to keep up a romantic correspondence with their sweetheart back home, only to find that she had dropped them for someone else. Separation also put an immense strain on marriages. Lieutenant Harwood, held captive in Eichstatt, considered himself fortunate for being single and only having his parents to correspond with.

The intimacies of one's private affairs were discussed to a far greater extent than would ever have been the case in normal life. There were numerous cases of officers whose wives admitted unfaithfulness in their letters and demanded their freedom. I suppose the war years were too long and, human nature being what it is, there were bound to be instances such as these; but I often wondered if the wives at home would not have been a little less outspoken in their letters if they had stopped to think for one moment of the effect these confessions must have on their husbands. No one who has not been a POW can begin to realise the utter misery, helplessness and feeling of frustration that such news can bring.

Families were advised by the Joint War Organisation and others to be careful when writing letters to their prisoner of war, so as not to appear too happy. To extol the virtues of a recent fine meal or trip to the seaside might result in the recipient feeling particularly frustrated that they couldn't share in such pleasures. While contact with home might bring great happiness to a prisoner, the reverse could also be true; reminders of home comforts may bring sadness, depression and despair. But it wasn't so much what was said in letters that could affect the prisoner of war most – it was more often than not just holding in one's hands a piece of paper which only a few weeks before had been in the possession of their loved one. This reinforced the idea that the physical act of exchanging a letter was just as important as its content. Such a notion was perhaps just as well for a prisoner such as Frank Stewart, who was finding letter-writing a definite challenge.

Either I've got a lot to say and there's not enough room, or (much more commonly) I've got nothing to say and there's too much. Letter writing is difficult under these conditions where the most interesting or amusing incidents in an otherwise monotonous existence are usually uncensorable. Also, I can't give any true impression of life here with all its various aspects in so short a space.

Communication with home was all-important to prisoners of war and despite the concerns which Frank Stewart described, the process of exchanging correspondence and receiving parcels was invaluable to maintaining morale within the community of the camp. Even those who did not receive mail were able to experience enjoyment in sharing news with their fellows, or appreciating the shared contents of parcels. However, the need remained for prisoners to establish more regular and reliable pastimes to keep themselves both busy and entertained.

4 | Entertainment

The drab monotony of that life... seemed to open my eyes and make me see the small and commonplace things of the world for the first time

With boredom being the main characteristic of prisoner of war life, it therefore followed that efforts to alleviate their regular monotony would be uppermost in the minds of captives. They would have to rely on their own ingenuity and organisational skills in order to provide themselves with forms of entertainment. When Eric Monckton arrived at Marlag-Milag Nord he was very impressed by the facilities already in existence there for the amusement of the prisoner of war community.

When I entered the camp, the Merchant Navy Concert Party was in full swing and had been granted a large disused barrack hut as a theatre, very good plays being put on and the dresses obtained from the now disused Bremen Theatre or made in the camp by the prisoners. The band of the RMS Orama, *who were captured, had their instruments replaced by the Red Cross and were in full swing at concerts and the Merchant Navy theatre. Occasional Nazi propaganda films were shown, the large community dining hall being chiefly used for these occasions. Football, cricket, baseball, skating in the winter, boxing bouts and sports days were very well attended as a diversion from the monotonous day by day lot of the prisoners. The Sports Committee, under a Captain Hill, was responsible for most of the sporting events that took place and they certainly did well for all the prisoners who were no doubt very thankful for their efforts in that line. The large sports ground at the southern edge of the camp was opened up shortly after I arrived and it was a large ground being able to have a football match, cricket match and a baseball pitch all going at the same time, if wanted so. The ground was outside the original barbed wire boundary of the southern end of the camp and was itself contained in the usual 12-feet-high barbed wire fencing. A daily round of sport was soon under way after the sports ground was opened, and providing the weather was good. The only drawback to everything that happened in the camp was the eternal fencing-in by the wire and the presence at all times of the Nazi guards. One could never forget that one was cooped up like a lot of hens in a fowl house, and it tended to put a dismal effect on everything that took place.*

One of the most popular forms of entertainment for prisoners of war proved to be sport, as arguably the best means of relieving pent-up aggression and emotion. Physical exertion also provided an excellent way to keep fit, although the relatively small amounts of food available to those in captivity ensured that nobody would be gaining weight. Sport also proved popular with the Italians and Germans, who liked to watch it and encouraged the pastime as a way to keep the prisoners occupied and out of trouble. The captors could also remove the privilege, if so required, as a form of punishment. Although consistently popular as a pastime, the enthusiasm for sporting activity did vary according to the prisoners' rations; little food of poor quality meant that few could summon up the appetite for extended physical exertion. However, it was often the case that detailed football and rugby seasons were put together and enjoyed, complete with league tables, while inmates in Colditz

Castle even arranged their own Olympics. Prisoners in Stalag Luft III at Sagan formed their own golf club. Sports equipment such as footballs, cricket bats and board games were sent out to prisoners by the YMCA and the Red Cross. Indeed, sporting activities undertaken by prisoners could range from the standard outdoor pursuits such as football, rugby or cricket to indoor pastimes as sedate as chess or dominoes or as harsh as boxing or wrestling. Among the more dignified forms of exercise was that practised by Frank Stewart.

Walking is the commonest exercise, of course, and at the moment I'm doing five rounds a day which comes to about four miles. But exercise isn't the only reason for walking. It affords privacy. I've mentioned before how lacking we are in privacy and the best way of overcoming it is by walking, either alone or with one other person. The Greek sophists always favoured perambulation when discussing the higher things and they were right. Not that I discuss the higher things much, but walking does seem to help to loosen the tongue and all my most interesting and enjoyable conversations have taken place while walking round the camp.

For practical reasons, some hobbies and pastimes could not be easily followed in a prisoner of war camp, yet prisoners could still write about and debate their interests with like-minded comrades. Captives in Stalag IV-B formed the Mühlberg Motor Club, which produced their own magazine called *Flywheel*, each copy uniquely written and drawn by hand. A typical issue might describe car journeys before the war, illustrations of futuristic cutting-edge vehicles, and motoring advice all put together largely from memory. Magazines such as this were routinely handed around from one prisoner to another, or lent out in the manner of a library book, yet their longterm retention not only during the war but for many years afterwards indicates the importance that their creators and readers attached to them.

The nature of captivity also lent itself to quiet contemplation and reading, with most camps allocating space for a reading room or library. The Indoor Recreations Section of the Red Cross and Order of St John was set up in the autumn of 1940 and by the end of the war had sent out 239,500 books to prison and internment camps in Europe. Similarly, the YMCA sent over half a million books on behalf of the United States Red Cross. The choice of books dispatched had to be made very carefully, with anything containing maps or information that might help an escape attempt requiring censorship if it was not outright banned. Some authors were deemed unsuitable by the German authorities, such as notable Jewish writers or authors whose political views were regarded as incompatible with National Socialism. Occasionally books could slip through the censorship net, however, with works such as *My Early Life* by Winston Churchill proving a popular choice among readers. Classic fiction was always popular, but also factual books were much sought after on subjects such as art, music, history and biography. Travel writing and books concerning English country life were particularly popular for sentimental reasons and reinforced the notion that, for prisoners of war, reading provided an escape from the confines of the camp, if only via their imaginations. Philosophy was also very popular, with captivity allowing the men the opportunity for intellectual self-reflection in a manner that regular life largely did not. Officers' camps tended to have the largest libraries, since the prisoners there had greater opportunity for reading. Oflag VII-B at Eichstatt, where Frank Stewart was held, could boast a massive collection of books by the end of the war.

No prisoner, I suppose, can deny that he has read more and over a wider field in prison than he would have done at home, even if there hadn't been a war on. In effect, of course, from this point of view prison has been to many a university, that is a continuation of their education; for myself definitely so, since it was just another step after

Oxford. The delight has been that I could read when and what I liked and as a result I have gained the most perfect enjoyment from reading. I now realise that before the war I hardly read a thing and I now regret it. The library has increased gradually and is now up to 12,000 books, about a third of which are so-called technical as opposed to fiction. In addition every officer has a bookshelf of his own books so that in the whole camp there must be at least 50,000 books, supplied from private parcels or through the Red Cross. Not a bad source to draw from. In the four and a half years I find I've read about 350 of them or more than one and a half a week, but I'm a slow reader and I know one man who has passed the thousand mark.

An important part of recreational reading was the educational element, as prisoners were often keen to use the time at their disposal to learn new things and even work towards some form of recognised qualification. The Red Cross formed an Educational Books Section which worked directly with prisoners in order to provide them with educational resources. A panel of experts was convened in order to provide advice on appropriate books to send for particular subjects, while donations of books from universities, publishers or authors were encouraged as well as from the wider public. The King and Queen donated 1,700 books for Christmas in 1941. The demand from prisoners of war was huge, with the section receiving over 15,000 requests for educational books by the end of May 1942, to which they sent almost 70,000 books in response.

Linked with this desire for study and self-improvement, prisoners gave lectures on topics of which they had personal knowledge, with many such presentations proving to be of a high academic standard. In some camps, faculties were set up to encourage learning, with timetabled lectures complemented by a well-stocked library. Some prisoners chose to study just for study's sake or to fill the time; others trained with the intention of pursuing a career after the war. Professional bodies were persuaded to recognise exams sat within prisoner of war camps, many of which were the equivalent of Honours Degrees. Many different subjects and disciplines were covered, with 11 prisoners even sitting the ordination exam recognised by the Church of England. Paper for recording the examinations remained very hard to come by and charitable donations were relied upon to provide the requisite forms. Also, all such exam papers had to be checked by both the German and British censors. Over the course of the war, examination papers were sent to just under 17,000 candidates who took nearly 11,000 exams, the pass rate being an impressive 78.5 per cent. However, it could sometimes prove difficult to study or read, since a quiet spot was not always readily available in a confined location with limited facilities. Second Lieutenant Frank Stewart was one of many officers who studied for exams, but found that working for them was far from easy.

To begin with there are only two rooms in the camp where there is guaranteed silence. In these silence rooms there are benches and tables, but they are so close that once they are full it is impossible to move about without clambering over a few complaining bodies. There are 6 people to each table and each room can take 40–50 people. In summer you can hardly breathe. In winter you have to sit in a greatcoat. Added to that the fact that there is never real silence (there's always at least one person stamping in and out in hob-nailed boots) and you get a pretty exact picture. The only other trouble is that when there are exams on they use one of the silence rooms to take them in and the only certain way of getting a seat in the other one is to get up at 7am (not that I do, of course). But I don't think the benefit of these silence rooms can be exaggerated. I honestly believe that without them a far larger number of people would have gone off their head. There are admittedly a few who sit there all day and every day and as a result of it <u>have</u> practically gone off their head, but to many it has been a place of relief. Quiet is a *thing we get little of and then only when you least expect it, and to know that at a particular moment you <u>can</u> go somewhere to work in peace, if not in complete quiet, is a great benefit, not only to those working for exams.*

The natural bedfellow to reading and studying was writing, and many prisoners devoted considerable time and thought to the notion of keeping a diary or written record of their captivity. Few managed to maintain a regular written account, often down to their initial enthusiasm dissipating due to the regularity and monotony of camp life, but simple diary notes might form the basis for a later memoir, written up in detail after liberation. Notebooks inscribed 'A Wartime Log' were issued to many British prisoners of war by the YMCA during the final year or so of the conflict; similar books had already been presented by Canadian and American charities. The idea was to encourage the men to use the log book in order to keep a diary, make sketches, store recipes, write poetry or collect autographs. There was also space to hold photographs or postcards, and even a small envelope pocket to keep mementos or souvenirs. Many surviving examples of the YMCA log books contain some excellent sketches that show scenes in their respective camps, and many talented prisoners would devote considerable time to drawing and painting. As with reading and writing, the temptation was for the men to reflect on imagined scenes of peacetime, with artistic depictions of the green fields of England proving very popular as a subject.

Frank Stewart and some of his comrades in Oflag VII-B took up another pastime – knitting.

As early as 1941 Harold and I decided to make use of the small knowledge we'd had drummed into us at our respective kindergartens and set about knitting a pair of socks from wool retrieved from other worn-out socks. Harold produced most of the theory and I most of the practice. We worked entirely from another old pair, stitch by stitch, and the result was quite satisfactory. At that time we were two of the few who had descended to something so unmanly and I don't suppose there were more than a dozen or so knitters in the camp. By the end of 1942 we had many disciples and pullovers began to be made. A number of rivals grew up and during the winter of 1942–1943 the woollen hat came into fashion, the various models showing that several different 'schools' had been set up. The climax was reached last winter when about two-thirds of the camp took to the business and a sort of standard prisoner's pullover was evolved on the three strand principle which was warm, thick and easily made in a comparatively short space of time.

Other forms of crafting existed in the same camp.

There are two other minor crafts which I must mention as, though the workers are few, the benefit to the camp is very great. There are two watchmakers who sit by a window all day repairing watches. They have a few tools sent from home and from Switzerland and though the trouble is spare parts they have carried out innumerable repairs of all kinds. Everyone is very grateful to them for they have devoted two years of their lives to the common good without any complaint. The other small group are the four officers who make false teeth. We have always been lucky with our dentists who have never had a chance of competing with the amount of work to be done (the diet is not conducive to good teeth) and they have got through an incredible amount of first class work. There are only two of them but they deal with about 20 patients a day. Under them are the false teeth makers who started up work about a year ago and have already satisfied many clients.

With England once being described as a nation of gardeners, it is perhaps not surprising that gardening became a popular pastime for British prisoners in those camps where the facilities allowed it. Gardening just for pleasure was pursued, with flowers bringing brightness to the borders of even the dullest parade ground, but prisoners also devoted time to growing their own fruit or vegetables. By early 1943, the Red Cross had sent 456 parcels of vegetable seeds and 196 containing flower seeds to 67 camps. Manure to help them grow was obtained from the horse dung regularly deposited by transport animals passing through the camp. The Royal Horticultural Society sent textbooks via the Red Cross's Educational Books Section and allowed prisoners of war to sit its examinations. Eric Monckton observed the value of this particular pastime.

Gardening formed a diversion for many and there were many parts of the camp allotted to it. Seeds were brought in from outside by the workers or could be purchased from the canteen, out of the 10 or 20 Reichmarks per month that the British Government allowed each prisoner out of his allowance of wages paid by them to his relatives or accumulated for him at home until his return. The results of this gardening effort was indeed good and there were grown tomatoes, onions, lettuce, cabbage, beetroot and many other vegetables – all very much to the benefit of the growers. The only difficulty was the carrying of buckets of water from the few pumps laid on in the camp. Flower patches were very grand and there was indeed in the summer a large variety of flowers grown.

This floral appreciation extended to the local fauna too. Bird watching proved another popular pastime and led to a significant demand for published guides to be sent from home, illustrating the different kinds of bird to be seen in Europe. Indeed, prisoner of war life in captivity often led to a much greater awareness and appreciation of one's surroundings, as recognised by Lieutenant Harwood.

I shall always be thankful for those years as a POW in one respect. The drab monotony of that life and the continual pangs of hunger seemed to open my eyes and make me see the small and commonplace things of this world for the first time. I saw fresh beauty in the most ordinary flowers – flowers one had always taken for granted – and the colouring of the trees in their spring foliage was more vivid than I had ever known it. I watched the movement of ants and small insects with all-absorbing interest. I was not alone in this appreciation of everyday things; I saw a marked fondness for animals and birds. We were not allowed to keep dogs but the Germans permitted cats in the camp to keep down the rats and mice. Before many months had passed at Eichstatt there must have been at least 200 cats in the camp. It is true that they were sometimes killed and eaten by a few of the more hungry prisoners but for the most part they were cared for and fed out of our meagre rations. I am sure that most of the owners of the cats probably disliked these animals in normal life – not many men love cats – but here was something upon which they could lavish affection. The cats were only incidental; anything else would have done.

For most adults in the 1940s, smoking was an essential part of relaxation. Everybody smoked cigarettes or pipes and, in an era largely ignorant of the health dangers attached to the habit, it was seen as very unusual to abstain. With tobacco still regarded as an essential requisite for human wellbeing, the Red Cross sent each man a ration of 50 cigarettes a week (or 2 oz of tobacco) with a special double delivery at Christmastime. It has been estimated that almost 1.5 billion cigarettes were sent to Italy and Germany via the International Committee of the Red Cross between 1941 and March 1945. Alternatives to tobacco which were sometimes adopted by prisoners when supplies of real cigarettes dried up included desiccated leaves and tree bark, perhaps wrapped in a thin page from a book. While not as effective as a proper smoke, such ersatz cigarettes at least gave the illusion of the real thing.

As well as being smoked for enjoyment, tobacco became an effective currency within prisoner of war camps. Sometimes a sophisticated 'swap shop' was set up in larger camps where the exchange rate for cigarettes was chalked up on a board and then used as a guide when swapping cigarettes for other goods or services. This exchange rate would fluctuate regularly, according to supply and demand. Services exchanged for a smoke might include preparing the day's food or cleaning the hut, and it was not unknown for cigarettes to be handled and bartered so much that they would finally deteriorate into something crumpled and dirty, far removed from their original appearance.

Cigarettes were also a valuable currency for gambling. Betting pools were not uncommon, often concerning themselves with bets on the war's progress while at other times devoted to sporting events, either real or imagined, held in the camp. Predictions on when hostilities may end was a common focus, while elaborate 'horse race meetings' would be organised, with the roll of a die deciding the winner. Card games were also eternally popular, with ongoing poker and bridge tournaments being a regular occurrence. Marlag-Milag Nord was a positive den of gambling, according to Eric Monckton.

Gambling was very much in evidence, and there was a hall close to the main gate, which was converted into a gambling den at nights. It was one of the usual large barracks used as a crew's dining hall for the ratings. Every Wednesday and Saturday night horse and dog racing were held, an elaborate and very good system of track with all the appearance of a real but miniature meeting, being made by one of the officers. What with the 'tote' bookies, race commentator, and the organization for dealing with the betting and the actual races, the hall on these occasions was a hive of industry. Reichmarks were the monies used for bets, and some of the prisoners came away with hundreds of Reichmarks when lucky. Betting sidelines such as Sunshine Wheel, poker, crap, 'The Beans' and roulette were also in vogue there. Sometimes there was a raid made by the Germans, who considered it not within the Prisoner of War Conventions rules, but it survived these raids and flourished for the fortunate few that ran it. One famous lucky 'millionaire', a Japanese who claimed British nationality called Taki, must have coined in thousands of Reichmarks from fellow prisoners.

Another somewhat illicit pleasure much missed by prisoners of war was alcohol. Some took it upon themselves to distil their own 'hooch' by various ingenious means, but the effect of such potent drink on men who had involuntarily abstained from alcohol for quite some time could lead to unforeseen consequences, as Wilfred Sutton recalled.

Some of the boys had made a most powerful brew from raisins and potatoes. It was decided to keep it for the right occasion which in fact was the New Years Eve of 1944. At that time our basic diet was three small potatoes and one piece of black bread per day. You can imagine the effect of this brew on weakened stomachs. In no time the boys were 'Brahms and List'. Well we in the theatre were called upon to give a cabaret and my part together with a South African chum named Bruce Coombes was to dance a tango. Dancing was my hobby and Bruce was the South African champion. He dressed as a Gaucho and I dressed as a rather gorgeous gypsy girl. We impressed our audience to more than the normal degree because, [with] this most exotic dance, the effects of the booze and the music, I had many offers of a bed in the corner. As a result I grew my moustache.

Alcohol also commonly formed part of Christmas celebrations, such as the occasion of Christmas Day 1944 at Lindau, described by Eric Laker.

Last night I was paralytic! Had about a tumbler full of Schnapps (bought from a Czech for 70 cigarettes) and some home-made fire-

water. I was absolutely and completely under the influence. In other words blind drunk! I regret to say I can remember nothing after drinking the Schnapps, but I am told I was determined to do a dance on the red hot stove, but was eventually led away to bed, in company with several other inebriates. Amos Pellen (who had just returned from hospital after having his right hand amputated) swore that every time he went out into the air someone hit him behind the knees with a cricket bat, causing him to fall down. I cannot say. I could see nothing. What a Christmas party! I discovered that the Schnapps I had been drinking was pure alcohol, made from wood. If you drink much you go blind, and if you drink a lot more, well, one just snuffs it.

In some camps, as Eric Monckton recalled, distilling alcohol became such an enterprise that it recalled the days of prohibition America, when illicit stills would be raided and secret alcohol parties held.

In the camp were also some enterprising prisoners, said to be the apprentices in a barrack, who went in for distilling alcohol. This was a constitution-destroying product made from prunes, raisins and potatoes. When these were in short supply they lit upon the way of producing it from boot-blacking. The result of this distilling was that several men were placed in hospital with nervous trouble, blindness, etc. It was a much despised 'racket' and the cause of the Gestapo search raids, but the distilling still went on, despite these raids for the 'stills'. Greater efforts should have been made to stop this beastly 'racket'. However, the greater majority of prisoners managed to keep away from this alcohol habit and it was only indulged in by the very few ratings that could not help themselves to avoid it.

About this time there occurred the only bit of bad trouble I saw in the camp between the prisoners, and caused through the distilling of alcohol. It happened in the American and Canadian ratings barrack, starting off with an insult thrown out and ending in a free rough house when an African or West Indian drew a razor across the throat of one of the Americans, causing a deep and bad wound. The razor just missed cutting the man's jugular artery by a fraction of an inch, the prominent figure in this act being one of the camp's boxing champions. He had turned out a nuisance in the camp with his drinking bouts and insults to anyone he saw. He was taken out of the camp and placed in the 'off-lager' jail, the injured man being treated in the camp hospital. A movement was started to definitely stop all the distilling of alcohol and to have all the rough element moved out of the camp. The Nazis, however, made lots of promises and there the matter stopped as far as they were concerned.

One of the most widespread forms of entertainment to be seen in prisoner of war camps, however, was also one of the most simple – music. Commonly enjoyed by everybody and beneficial to raising one's spirits or encouraging relaxation, music was also welcomed by the Germans and Italians as a pastime which could not obviously benefit anything illicit, such as attempts to escape. As prisoner numbers increased, so too did the likelihood of each camp benefitting from persons who could play instruments or sing. The Indoor Recreations, Fiction, Music and Games Section of the Red Cross sent out parcels of simple instruments such as mouth organs or flutes, although requests from prisoners for specific instruments were also followed up wherever possible. By the end of the war, over 16,000 musical instruments had been posted out to prisoners in this way, together with musical scores and books and orchestral combinations for a hundred camps. Some professional musicians had managed to keep their own instruments after being captured, or were able to purchase some while in captivity, either legitimately or through the common bartering and bribery system practised with the guards. For those prisoner of war camps without access to instruments or lacking the facilities to accommodate orchestras, the British armed forces'

Entertainments National Service Association (ENSA) made recordings available on gramophone records on a monthly basis which were delivered via the YMCA.

Alan Bolt had been serving as a signalman with the King's Royal Rifle Corps in North Africa when he was taken prisoner early in 1942. A skilled musical composer before the war, he was confined to various camps in Italy, including PG51 at Altamura where his professional skills would be called into use, initially as part of the church choir.

The arrival of some padres in the camp increased the demand for church music, so the choir got more ambitious and produced the odd anthem from time to time to tunes which had to be rearranged from peoples' memory or composed by me as required. From that, the move to include secular music in the choir's repertoire was inevitable, and we joined with Frank Lazari's five-piece jazz band to produce some entertainment in the camp. We had rigged up a kind of boxing-ring stage in the compound, and this provided a place for various entertainments. By this time the choir was about 14 to 16 strong and I was able to get some who had experience of singing in shows and concerts to sing words and tunes to me so that I could then arrange them for the choir. Spirituals, folk songs, ballads – all came to be arranged. We also gradually acquired instruments, and the band expanded to about 20 in strength and included a sufficient variety of instruments to make it possible to play selections from musicals such as the Quaker Girl, *various Ivor Novello shows, piano scores of which became available, together with individual songs such as* The Fishermen of England *and also items from* Merrie England *and the Gilbert and Sullivan operas. I was invited to conduct the orchestra and, of course, to score the music, little of which came in orchestral arrangements. One particularly successful item was an arrangement of* Funiculi Funicula *for choir and orchestra, which the Italians liked so much that the whole camp was awarded extra rations the next day!*

Luckily, Bolt's interest in orchestration went back a long way and was a natural result of being born to a musical family. His grandfather was a professional percussionist who had taught his grandson the skills of drumming from the age of three. Bolt's musical work continued when transferred to the German camp of Stalag IV-B at Mühlberg.

Our captors were particularly impressed by one of our concerts and this led to me being placed in a difficult situation. I was sent for by the German Kommandant and offered the chance to go to Dresden and be involved in the world-famous Opera and conduct the orchestra there. I knew that this would turn into a propaganda exercise and I turned down the offer, making it plain that I considered it my duty to provide entertainment for our own people in the camp. A few days later I was sent for again, and this time it was an officer from the SS who was sitting at the desk. He then questioned me about this 'nonsense' of refusing the opportunity they were offering me. I stood my ground, and eventually he curtly dismissed me. I heard no more about it, but it was not a pleasant experience. Incidentally, if I had accepted the offer I may well have perished in the bombardment of Dresden which took place shortly afterwards!

The natural affiliate to musical performances was the theatre, which became one of the most popular and widespread forms of entertainment performed in prisoner of war camps. This might take the shape of revues featuring comedy and singing, humorous performances based on the old British tradition of pantomime, or 'straight' theatrical dramas. The reason that theatre was so popular was that almost every man could be involved in some way. If not performing on the stage itself as an actor, singer, comedian or musician, a prisoner could work behind the scenes as a carpenter, electrician, tailor, or scenery artist. Stage productions provided the best example of how prisoner ingenuity could create something splendid out of very little indeed, and the opportunity to escape into the glamour of the theatre could help men to forget, if only for a brief period of time, the drudgery of their real-life circumstances.

Norman Wylie of the Royal Corps of Signals had been captured very early on in the war, at St Valery in France in 1940. Now serving as an interpreter at Stalag XX-B located near Willenberg, Wylie was keen to set in motion some sort of theatrical entertainment for the camp, but initially found that such an activity was far from a priority for either the prisoners themselves or their captors.

Theatrical entertainment began, like everything else, in a small way. As a matter of fact it didn't exist at all in 1940, owing to the fact that the men had more important things to think about – food, clothing, blankets and all the ordinary requirements of a simple though unpleasant existence. But in March of 1941, the first organised concert, on a stage of four tables, was given in the library which could hold about 200 uncomfortably. The programme, to which both French and English contributed, consisted mostly of musical items and one or two sketches. When summer of 1941 came and it was felt that the war would not be 'over by Christmas', the staging of camp concerts became a major consideration since they would contribute largely to mitigating the boredom experienced by all ranks behind the wire.

A request to the German authorities for a concert hut or proper resources for staging a show was outright refused.

Entertainment was definitely not encouraged at that time. Instead there were German lessons going on most evenings, but these were promptly left unattended when the thin wedge of propaganda began to thrust itself in. However, nothing ventured, nothing gained. We proceeded to make the best of things for the time being, extending the platform by adding the library forma and rigging up wings, a curtain and adding footlights and overhead battens. Every appliance, every gadget, was difficult to get and had to be begged, borrowed or stolen – mostly the latter. Our great standby at this juncture was crepe paper – for dresses, for curtains, for scenery. Between us, the French and ourselves, we cleared out all the stocks of this commodity in town as our programmes grew more ambitious. We also had to buy make-up, electric bulbs, cardboard for posters and tickets.

In other camps, prisoner theatre often began in even more primitive circumstances, as Wilfred Sutton recalled. As a flight engineer with a pathfinder unit, he had bailed out of his Halifax bomber over Hannover during the first of their Berlin raids, was captured and taken to Stalag IV-B at Mühlberg in September 1943. This was shortly before Alan Bolt's arrival, which would boost the musical provision in that camp. The camp library already happened to include the published text of a few plays, and the prisoners therefore decided to enact them as best they could.

We had no facilities in these days but we used to put up a blanket in the centre of the hut and with the aid of a sound effects man we read the play to our audience. It was just like listening to a radio play, I remember that R.C. Sherriff's Journey's End *was one of these plays. We did entertain the lads this way and it was well as far as it went but it certainly did not go far enough and eventually through our Man of Confidence and the major who was our senior officer, we did persuade our captors to let us have a part of a hut to be made into a theatre... with the aid of a lick of paint, a bit of timber and a few blankets and sheets we opened it as IV-B's Camp Theatre in April.*

Other camps had already established an ongoing entertainment schedule centred around their theatrical facilities. Norman Wylie remembered how revues were presented on the Stalag XX-B library stage in September and November 1941.

By now, Christmas was not far off and it behove us to prepare some sort of pantomime. There were difficulties in the way, of course – no script, no topical numbers, no proper costumes, plus inadequate staging facilities. Pantos need fairly large casts. It didn't make matters easier when the cast of these shows had to dress in a separate barrack and get to the stage by crossing muddy patches of ground and clambering through a window... I wrote out a script in which Aladdin, Prince Charming, Babes in the Wood and Red Riding Hood all managed to meet, and called it Babes in the Wood. *Just as production was in full swing, a most unfortunate thing happened. There was a typhoid scare in the town and we were all confined to camp. That wasn't so bad, but on the German doctor's orders, we had all to get our hair closely cropped. This was a calamity. It wouldn't be very romantic to see Prince Charming making love in such a defenceless condition. However, 'the show must go on'. It eventually opened about the middle of January, and despite all difficulties, enjoyed a great success. Hair, though short, was at least presentable [after] about four weeks of cultivation and massage.*

What began as primitive amateur dramatic shows could sometimes develop into elaborate theatrical spectaculars. Stalag 383 at Hohenfels, for instance, could boast two stages with several hundred seats, meaning that each of the 6,000 prisoners in the camp was able to enjoy a show every fortnight. Collecting together costumes for the productions could prove difficult, however, as appears to have been the case for Wilfred Sutton and his comrades at Stalag IV-B.

Any form of disguise, every piece of civilian clothing, every shirt or anything that looked like a shirt was of use to the camp escape committee. It was of course the duty of POWs to try to escape, for which civilian clothing was a must. So all we could muster for the theatre was, as far as the Germans were concerned, a security risk. We had to do some very hard selling to convince them that our wardrobe would be kept for the theatre and would not be part of the escape committee. Anyway we did this and we had a stage, we had some property and a limited wardrobe. We also had a little bit of makeup, a prompt box, an orchestra and because of the talent at our disposal we were able to form a complete entertainments section. We each ran a two week show, which meant as far as the drama group was concerned we worked as Rep. We would be performing one play, rehearsing a second and casting a third. In every six weeks we were able to put on a play. Once again, whilst properties and the wardrobe were not easily available, there were always German guards or French prisoners who worked outside the camp who, for the right fee, could get what we needed. The fee was cigarettes which became the only exchange throughout the camp. Cigarettes were, of course, in very short supply but we obtained them by charging admission. I cannot remember the details of the fee but it was something like 3 cigarettes in the orchestra stalls, working down to 1 cigarette for the back stalls and the theatre held about 120 people. Exchange rates, as in our civilian times, varied according to supply and demand but I think our prices were constant.

A further problem faced when staging productions was how to fill the parts usually played by women. The answer, of course, was for male prisoners to impersonate females as best they could. Perhaps bearing in mind the audience's overwhelming desire to see 'real' women, this cross-dressing was, on the whole, carried out in a very tasteful and considerate way, rather than the camp drag act that might be more easily imagined. Wilfred Sutton stressed how such versatility was absolutely essential to putting on a successful show.

Our first major production was a musical revue called Music in the Cage. *The plot, such as it was, revolved about British troops on leave in Cairo. Amongst other requirements, we had to find a dozen gorgeous dancing girls. Some of them were smashers. They were headed by a Canadian named Garfield Townley, who made such a super harem girl he was immediately nicknamed 'Sugar', a name which stuck to him for the rest of his days in camp. Of course, we had a very big advantage against civilian amateur or even professional productions as we had, without making too much of a pun, a captive audience. This meant that the theatre was packed for each performance and as they had been without entertainment for over six months the show was an absolute 'Wow'. We were followed by the variety people who also were a success and they in turn were followed by the orchestral section. We had by now one or two really good 'females' who could also act serious parts which overcame our biggest difficulty. One of our female impersonators was a married man with a child and how his wife and family felt about him when he got back home I hardly dare to think. He had practised and developed female behaviours to an Nth degree. He had shaved under his arms, shaved his legs and forearms, sat like a woman and could have fooled anyone when he was dressed like a woman.*

Convincing costumes were an essential part of any production, and Norman Wylie recalled the challenges in putting together a varied wardrobe for Stalag XX-B's theatrical performances.

When I think of those early days in the library it must certainly have been a test of endurance for all concerned. Swiss Spring is noteworthy for the fact, however, that for the first time we went to sources other than crepe-paper for our dress material. Old blankets were cut up and made into costumes, trousers, jackets. Bits of sacking came in handy; odd pieces of cloth were borrowed or requisitioned, and under the expert scissors of some of our tailors, the most wonderful creations came before the footlights. Hats, Parisian style, were cut out of cardboard and adorned with flowers. The great problem, of course, was stockings and shoes. Odd stockings were sometimes procurable for coffee or cigarettes,

*but the feet had to be cut off before they would fit our 'heroines' and
they invariably had ladders in them. And I don't think anything was
more visible to our audiences <u>than</u> those stockings, or, shall I say,
legs. They seemed to catch the full glare of the footlights and the
undivided attention of the audience. Ladies' shoes were practically
non-existent, even to our foraging parties. We made sandals out
of odd scraps of leather, with medium heels of wood and painted
them in vivid greens, blues or reds all according to the colour of
the costume. We borrowed, however, quite a few accessories such
as shoes, hats and handbags from the French, as they seemed to
have a flare for that sort of thing. So, gradually, we were beginning
to build up a wardrobe of sorts. Wigs we could always hire from a
shop in town. Cheap jewellery could also be bought. Anything that
could be lifted from the town by working parties – bits of cloth,
scarves, 'kerchiefs for example – came our way. The word 'steal'
was eradicated from the POW's vocabulary.*

Unbelievably, Wylie was able to obtain professional costumes for
their performance of *Cinderella*.

*I asked permission to go to the city of Danzig for costumes. We
had such a large cast that we could not possibly find the material
to clothe them all, not to mention the time that would be involved
to make the clothes. A lorry from our camp went every so often to
a French POW camp in Danzig with a load of private parcels from
home for the prisoners there, and occasional passengers went with
it. I asked to travel with the lorry to a form of theatrical costumers,
from whom the French had already hired costumes. After a great
deal of official coming and going, I was given the permission,
provided a German interpreter went with me. This was reasonable
enough, of course. One fine morning I set off for the Free City, not
so free any longer, and that night I returned to camp with four cases
of costumes. I may add that the transaction had been considerably*

eased by the passing of chocolate and soap over the counter after the attention of the interpreter had been momentarily diverted.

Through their regular parcel deliveries, the Red Cross supplied new scripts for the prisoners to perform. One production, *Outward Bound*, required a fireworks display as a crucial part of the story. But how on earth were the prisoners at Mühlberg expected to stage such a thing with the limited resources at their disposal?

It was very critical that this scene was really effective but you can imagine the headaches it gave us. We did in fact overcome them with a marvellous effect from the auditorium. The cellar steps were supposed to be off stage left and we rigged up a kaleidoscope of coloured papers which one of the effects men spun in front of a strong electric light. The sound effects people were making the appropriate bangs and whistles and two stage hands were lighting tapers and throwing these to each other in front of the coloured wheel, which as I said was behind a strong lamp. The effect of the sparks, the flame and the shadows was, together with the noise, really terrific, although a considerable fire hazard. We had to have two men standing by with buckets of water and sand in case of trouble but happily during the whole run nothing serious happened.

Such ingenuity ensured that theatrical productions of this nature were a roaring success among the prisoners. Indeed, many shows even managed to break through the language barrier and prove themselves of international appeal, as Norman Wylie observed.

Babes in the Wood *[was] scheduled for six nights, ran for nine. What amazed us was that it 'took' with the other nationalities in the camp, especially the Serbs. We gave a special performance for them, when a synopsis of the story was read out to them beforehand by their interpreter. Perhaps they hadn't seen anything quite like this before. They laughed uproariously when three of our chaps, dressed as fairies, executed a woodland dance; were awed when the villain lurched on to a green-lit stage; cheered when he was eventually dispatched by the prince in a duel, and broke into tremendous applause when, after a fanfare of trumpets, the princess, complete with crown, veil and crinoline advanced down stage on the arm of her bridegroom. Even awed Germans dropped in to see it. The censors too seemed to enjoy it. No show could go on, the script of which had not already been forwarded to Stalag Headquarters for scrutiny. Every page of script and every lyric had to bare the censor's stamp. Again, a censor had to be in attendance at every performance and the curtain could not rise without his presence. On occasions, we had to wait anything up to half an hour for him to arrive.*

Many theatrical performances had a particular appeal to their German captors. One of Wilfred Sutton's productions was set in Bavaria at the time of the Oktoberfest.

The news got to the German authorities and we had from the German commanding officer a request for a Command Performance. In those days all the German theatres were closed so even when they were on leave they had no entertainment. Our commanding officer was a man called Lieutenant Colonel Stossier who was a professional soldier but anti-Nazi in his outlook. Anyway on the first night he came along with his entourage and they were given the first row of the stalls for this Command Performance. I don't think we could charge them for their seats but they had a good time and congratulated us on our efforts.

But support from their German captors was not always enjoyed by prisoners in other camps, as Norman Wylie sadly noted.

The German Sergeant Major, who practically ran the camp, did <u>not</u> approve of our efforts. His only concern was to get as much work as he could out of each individual. We used to post sentries to keep a look out for him on his daily inspections round the camp, so that everything could be temporarily removed from sight.

Wylie proceeded to recall how the prisoners in Stalag XX-B managed to turn this German apathy towards their theatrical productions to good use, with their comedy revue *Jankers Away* which opened in August 1942.

The first night happened to coincide with the visit of our Protecting Power. The Swiss delegates, who understood English perfectly, enjoyed the show despite the terrific August heat, made more desperate by a packed audience. This was where our comedian got in quick, ad lib[bed] idiomatic cracks against Jerries, greatly to the amusement of the delegates. German officers, who were present but who didn't grasp our slang, laughed with their hosts, out of politeness I suppose. That made us laugh all the more – for nothing could have tickled the British sense of humour more than to see the unsuspecting Jerry taking a hearty laugh at himself.

Even for those camps which might lack theatre facilities or the necessary talent to stage productions, all was not lost. Most camps could claim to have a hidden wireless set, which provided news broadcasts by the BBC which could then be recounted around the camp. This news was often reported in a rather dramatic, theatrical way, as recollected by Lieutenant Frank Stewart.

Each evening one (or two) selected people listened to the news in some place unknown to anyone else. Half an hour later news readers from each block met together elsewhere and were given a summary which they later read out to members of their block before destroying their notes. On special occasions, such as a Churchill speech, notes were taken in shorthand and dictated to the news readers verbatim for further transmission. These moments were very absorbing and impressive. I remember the reaction of one prisoner who had listened, like us all, to a reading of the full text of a speech by King George VI. He remained silent for over a minute, and then said, 'That was a wonderful speech, wasn't it? There's only one thing that worries me about it, though. I always thought the King had a stutter.'

5 | Escaping

We painfully climbed the barbed wire fence.
We were free.

Prisoners of war sought to subvert the normal relationship of prisoner and captor at every opportunity, often refusing to conform to the expected rules of behaviour foisted on them. Small acts of rebellion were commonplace, ranging from bribing guards to stealing food, and these proved key to giving prisoners of war a degree of meaning to their existence. While small acts of insubordination or simple efforts to rile the guards were commonplace, the ultimate expression of this desire to cause trouble was to escape from captivity and seek a way back home, or at least to neutral territory. In this regard, the escape attempt was, in many ways, more important to the prisoner than their ultimate success. This is shown by the relatively small percentage of attempts which actually succeeded, since the vast majority failed to make it out of the confines of their camp. Throughout the Second World War there were around 21,500 British and Commonwealth prisoners of war across the world who managed to escape captivity and return to the Allied lines before the end of the conflict. This equated to less than half a per cent of the total number of prisoners of war worldwide. The chances of a successful escape were therefore very slim indeed, yet this did not deter prisoners from attempting to seek freedom by whatever means they could.

Almost all British officers held a belief that it was their duty, if captured, to attempt to escape. This expectation was commonly shared by non-commissioned soldiers too. Even if they should fail in the attempt, a considerable amount of enemy manpower would be diverted to catching and guarding the troublesome prisoner. The Geneva Conventions implied the legality of escape, yet a broad understanding was shared by most that any attempt should be made in as civil a manner as possible. Killing, hurting or even just striking a guard or a civilian in the process of escaping could still be considered a crime, both in the eyes of international law and local civilian justice. Prisoners of war remained subject to the holding power's laws but, theoretically at least, they were not subject to corporal punishment or excessive penalties. The maximum disciplinary penalty for an officer prisoner following their escape was 30 days solitary confinement, although incidences of theft or assault might lead to additional penalties.

It is important to remember that not all prisoners of war were desperate to escape. Many were already weary of the war and docile obedience until their liberation was an understandable desire. It might also prove to be the most prudent option when in the hands of an enemy who had already shown startling ruthlessness in many different ways. The worst examples of prison brutality in Germany were largely confined to the SS personnel who ran the concentration camps, yet some cruelty did also exist among the older veterans and infirm troops to be found in the regular guard garrisons. In addition, many prisoner of war camps operated a parole system, in which prisoners promised not to attempt to escape and in return enjoyed privileges such as escorted walks outside the camp or additional liberties. For some prisoners, this was by far the best option. Eric Monckton described a rare instance of such an expedition outside the grounds of Marlag-Milag Nord. We can only imagine the novelty of stepping outside the wire for those prisoners who had not experienced true freedom for such a long time.

> On 13th October [1944] I went for a walk with nine other captains and under guard escort. The only armament carried by this guard was a revolver, and all of us had to sign that we would not use this outing as an attempt to escape, it being pointed out to us that if such a thing occurred it would stop any future concession of outside walks for all the camp. From the camp we passed through the fir-tree woods to the south, then across fields in a westerly direction and near the village of Tarmstadt. There was a noticeable lack of bird life, probably due to the fir-trees which abound in this part, birds not liking the prickly branches and shoots for perching and nesting. In the woods and fields a deadly silence reigned everywhere. Later, our guard was approached as to the possibility of our doing an exchange of cigarettes for fruit, but he would have nothing to do in the matter as one of his guard friends had been given away by a farmer and he was put into jail for several days for allowing the prisoners to do it. On passing down a cart track, later on, we came on some farm workers – the farmer, five women and girls, a Frenchman and a couple of youths – all having their afternoon snack by the side of the field. They had a small pile of apples by their side and three of us who were some hundred yards behind the guard, went up and asked them if they had any to spare. I got ten large cooking apples and four eating ones for a tablet of soap, and as it was the first fresh fruit that I had had for some nine months, they were indeed very tasty and acceptable.

Even such occasional excursions as this from the confines of the camp were done under guard, and strict limitations remained. Any other opportunity for prisoners of war to see the wider world was usually limited to working parties travelling to sites to undertake labour, but this was far from an enjoyable experience. It was therefore understandable that, in some cases, the majority of a prisoner's time in captivity was spent considering how to escape the confines of their prison life.

It was statistically more likely for an officer to escape, perhaps reflecting the common understanding that they would be expected to do so as part of maintaining an honourable reputation. Yet the greatest number of escapes were actually by non-commissioned soldiers. If we look at the number of prisoners of war who successfully escaped through western Europe (including Switzerland), there were 3,087 successful 'home runs' by British other rank prisoners during the war, compared to 375 by British officers.

Putting aside the fact that there were proportionately a much greater number of other rank prisoners of war when compared to officers, it might also have been the case that non-commissioned prisoners could have been given greater opportunities to escape. Most other ranks held in Germany spent time working for their captors on farms or in mines, forest camps or industrial factories, often being sent from *Arbeitskommandos* (labour camps) attached to their main Stalag. Seven day working weeks were not unheard of. The strain of constant work in labour camps meant that for many the spirit to escape was simply not there, yet the environments they were placed in meant that there was often greater opportunity to escape when compared to officers held more securely in permanent camps. Any prisoner's chances of escape, however, whatever their situation, were largely down to a lucky opportunity arising as opposed to any particular cleverness to their plan. It should also be noted that many men made it successfully out of captivity only to be recaptured within a few hours or days.

The usual hope was to reach neutral territory such as Switzerland, Spain or Sweden, where the escaper would be able to make contact with the relevant Allied military attaché. Escapers arriving in a neutral country were free to move on, if they could, to their home country and continue fighting; evaders (those servicemen who had found themselves in enemy territory but had managed to avoid being taken prisoner) were supposed to be interned until the war's end. Many evaders therefore preferred to portray themselves as having escaped from captivity in order to avoid internment and reach home to fight once more.

There was much less chance of escape for prisoners of war in Italy than in Germany. Considering the 68,320 British, Commonwealth or Empire prisoners held in Italy by August 1943, only 602 escapes were attempted. Of these, only six men made it to safety. Why was this? Broadly speaking, the Italian guards were better at their job and more observant. Parcels were searched more thoroughly for potential escape aids, while British Intelligence had struggled to make contact with prisoners in Italian camps and so could not offer much external assistance. There was also another significant factor which acted against the success of any escape attempt in Italy. After breaking out of a camp in Germany, a prisoner of war could pose as a foreign worker, of which there were plenty. In Italy, however, foreigners were a rare sight and an undisguised fugitive would therefore stick out like a sore thumb.

Although considerable good fortune was required for any successful escape, the basis for a decent chance of making it home was to plan as much as possible in advance, as Eric Monckton recalled. Not least because of the need for identity documentation if the escaper was intending to travel any distance away from the camp.

Passports were necessary for anyone travelling from one district to another, even amongst the Nazi population. On the long distance trains there was always a Gestapo sentry who came round the train while on its journey and examined the passports of the travellers. Escapes were without a chance of success unless carefully planned out and the route and plan carried out to the letter. There was the case of a farm worker who stole a bicycle and proceeded off. He had no prearranged plan of escape and just pedalled along. After about

24 hours of journey on the bicycle, he finished up outside the camp, not so far from where he had started, and was more than surprised to find himself back again. That was just plain foolishness. Another case was where one of the escapees had got as far as Cologne and passed through the town when an air-raid was just beginning. He also had stolen a bicycle. He was so impressed with the intensity of the raid that occurred after he had passed through the place, that he turned round and rode in to see what damage was done. He was stopped and questioned while riding through the town for the second time, and taken into custody.

The actual process of getting out of the camp could be done in a number of ways: a tunnel might be dug covertly under the perimeter fence; a prisoner might create a fake uniform and disguise himself as a guard to walk out of the exit; or he might hide within a container or lorry in the hope of being carried out of the prison. The methods adopted by prisoners were both varied and ingenious. In order to allow the escaped prisoner as much time as possible to get clear of the camp before a search was undertaken, his remaining comrades would attempt to hide the fact that he had escaped. This would usually involve falsifying the head count at the regular roll calls (*appels*), which all prisoners were expected to attend. Sometimes good use could be made of 'ghosts', those prisoners whom the Germans wrongly believed to have left the camp sometime previously, but who could take the place of real escapers at roll calls.

While skill was certainly required in order to enact a successful escape – such as ingenuity in devising a plan, physical strength in surviving on the run, courage and audacity in bluffing one's way to freedom, language skills to avoid alerting the locals – there was an even greater element of pure luck involved. Many escapes depended on spur of the moment decisions, as Lieutenant Colonel Peter Brush found out. Adjutant of the 1st Battalion, Rifle Brigade at the time of his capture in France in June 1940, by the early summer of 1941

Brush was being held in Oflag V-B at Biberach, just under 70 miles from the Swiss border.

An opportunity arrived which I took advantage of. A German soldier dropped his pass outside the camp hospital, Dr Pollock picked it up and quickly brought it to me. It was copied by our forgers, roughly, in an hour and returned to the spot where Pollock had found it. Sometime later a worried looking soldier came peering along and, overjoyed, retrieved his pass. The forgers did a good job and Biberach Prisoner of War Camp passes 19, 20, 21 and 22 were produced. Seeing the difficulties in obtaining talc, paper, Indian ink, etc. we were ever grateful to them for their exacting work.

This would be the first stage to an audacious escape. Now that Brush had a fake pass to exit the camp, a cover story would also be required. Since he was unable to speak German, he decided to join forces with fellow prisoner Terence Prittie. Prittie was a fluent German speaker, having spent a year in Munich as a student, and would take on the challenge of bluffing their way past the initial sentries and any further soldiers they may encounter.

I was the dumb act, with 14 pounds of chocolate sludge, oatmeal and warm clothes concealed under my blue denims (Red Cross pyjamas, dyed blue, and given an outdoor appearance). I looked, as Terence has described, 'a hard bitten, paunch Great War veteran, puffing a German cigar'. If poked I could grunt. Terence was small, alert, blonde and a splendid young German awaiting his call-up. Our pending escape was known only by the Senior British Officer, our sentries and lookouts, and our devoted dressers who were as dedicated as if they were back stage in the theatre. Secrecy was important, as once people get to know anything, they immediately, without meaning to, give you away. I made one exception. I said to the senior New Zealand officer, 'Those Maori officers of yours,

Kr.=Gef. Offizierlager IX A   Ausgestellt: **Rotenburg/Fulda,**

~~Hauptlager~~

Zweiglager   am 23. SEPT 1943 194___

Kennkarte für Kriegsgefangene

Nur gültig für den Lagerbetrieb und in Verbindung mit der

Erk.-Marke Nr. 220_____

Dienstgrad: __Oblt._____

Name: ____Laing_____

Vorname: ____Walter Kenneth_____

23. OKT. 1943

Zur Beachtung!

Die Kennkarte dient als Ausweis der Krf. gegenüber den Organen der deutschen Lagerkommandantur. Sie ist wie die Erk.-Marke stets mitzuführen u. mit dieser auf Verlangen bei namentlichen Appells und beim Verlassen des Lagers vorzuweisen.

Verlust ist sofort zu melden.

Der Kommandant

Identity document issued to Lieutenant Walter Laing on arrival at Oflag IX-A/Z.

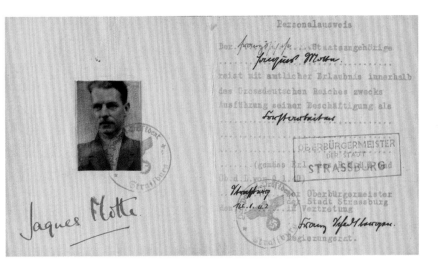

Opposite British prisoners at work in a quarry in the town of Laband, the base for working parties from Stalag VIII-B.

Top A forged identity document made in 1943 for an escape attempt by Lieutenant Ronald Eastman while he was a prisoner in Oflag VII-B, Eichstätt. He purported to be a French worker travelling through Germany.

Bottom A forgery kit used by Major Dick Woodley whilst he was a prisoner of war in Oflag IX-A, Rotenburg. As one of the camp's leading forgers, he made replica German stamps using rubber from the soles of army boots and managed to carve mirror-image German script for printing.

F/Lt QUAILE	F/Lt YOUNG
F/Lt DAWES	F/Lt CUNNINGHAM
F/Lt LANGDON	F/o PUTTICK
F/o MITCHELL	F/o JAMES
Lt HANLINE	Lt SNYDER
F/o MOYER	Lt STILLINGS

Menu

BREAKFAST
RAISIN JUICE
BARLEY-PORRIDGE, HONEY + CREAM
FRIED - BREAD + SPAM
TOAST + BLACKBERRY JAM
TEA

LUNCH
COLD HAM
WELSH RAREBIT
TARTINES KRIEGIEUX + CAFÉ au LAIT

TEA
ASSORTED SANDWICHES:-
(Cheese, Crab + Lobster, + Spam
Pâté, Peanut Butter + Jam)
CHRISTMAS CAKE
TEA

DINNER

POTAGE à la JULIENNE

SAUMON SUPÉRIEUR

TURKEY AMERICAN RÔTI
SPECIAL STUFFING   CHEF DAWES
POMMES RÔTIS   POMMES CREMES
CARROTTES   TURNIPS

CHRISTMAS PUDDING + CREAM

BISCUITS KRIEGIES avec FROMAGE

CANDY + NUTS

CAFÉ

SUPPER

HOT SAUSAGE ROLLS
ASSORTED SANDWICHES
TREACLE TART
HOT CHOCOLATE

XMAS EVE HOT MIDNIGHT SUPPER
BREAD + BUTTER OFF RATION

Clockwise from top left A photograph of the three 'Wooden Horse' escapers, taken shortly after their arrival in Stockholm (left to right: Michael Codner, Oliver Philpot, Eric Williams); British prisoners of war tend their garden at Stalag Luft III, Sagan; Sergeant Jack Diamond displays his manacled hands for the camera in a covert photograph taken to document evidence of German mistreatment of prisoners in Stalag VIII-B, Lamsdorf; A handmade Christmas 1944 menu from Stalag Luft III, Sagan, with its selection of food based largely on the shared contents of Red Cross food parcels.

Top Prisoners walking around one of the compounds in Stalag Luft III, Sagan.

Bottom A wireless radio receiver manufactured by Captain Ernest Shackleton at Oflag IX-A/Z, Rotenburg, using materials salvaged from the camp including cocoa tins and toothbrush handles.

Top A British concert party on stage during a performance given at Laband working camp, a satellite camp of the nearby Stalag VIII-B.

Bottom British concert party 'The Blue Jays' outside their hut in Stalag XXI-D, Pozna.

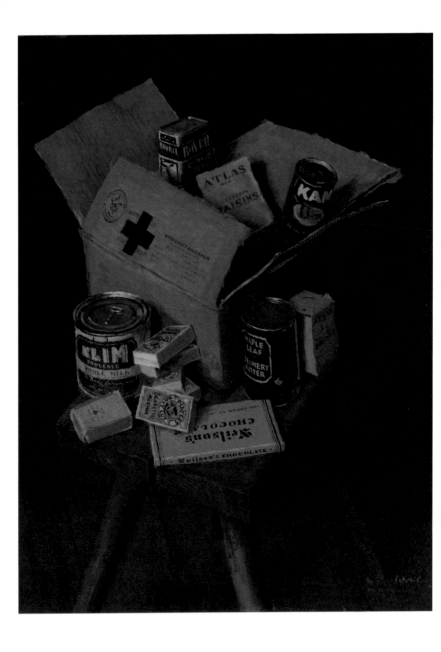

Above The Contents of a Red Cross parcel, painted by official war artist John Worsley in 1944.

Opposite top Two British boxers face each other in the ring at Stalag XXI-D, Pozna. A watchtower can be seen in the background.

Opposite bottom An impressive display by the prisoner of war gymnastics team at Stalag VIII-B.

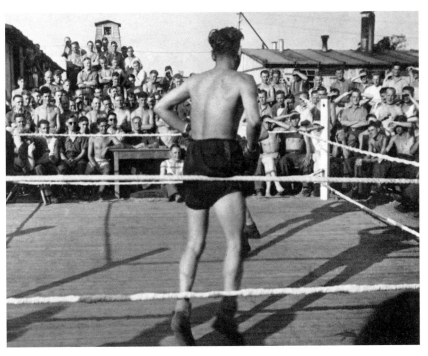

Top left In this official German photograph, staged for propaganda purposes, two German Flight Sergeants talk to British prisoners of war at Stalag Luft III, Sagan.

Clockwise, from top right These three clandestine photographs were taken secretly by Warrant Officer William Lawrence, an RAF prisoner of war in Stalag VIII-B, Lamsdorf. In order to conceal his camera from the German guards, Lawrence carried it in an old Red Cross box with a hole cut out for the lens. His images show prisoners busily opening their newly-received Red Cross parcels; the interior of a typical prisoner accommodation hut; and, in front of the watchtower, prisoners are sunbathing between lines of clothes and bedding hung out to air.

Left *Stabsfeldwebel* Gustav Rothenberger, known to the prisoners of war in Colditz as 'Franz Josef'.

Opposite top An aerial view of Colditz Castle, Oflag IV-C.

Opposite bottom Prisoners of war from Oflag IX-A/Z on the road between Dachrieden and Windeberg during their forced march east, 3 April 1945. A German officer, probably part of the camp staff, can be seen in the foreground with a bicycle.

The 'escape museum' in Colditz Castle, where the Germans displayed the equipment and fake uniforms used by prisoners who attempted to flee the Oflag.

Right The moment of liberation captured on film. British prisoners welcome the arrival of American troops at Oflag 79 in Brunswick, 12 April 1945.

Below Newly liberated British prisoners of war board planes for home at Brunswick, Germany, in April 1945.

Prisoners of war at Stalag XI-B near Fallingbostel on the day that they were liberated, 16 April 1945.

I am going out through the main gate at 11.16am tomorrow, could they do a war dance on the square in full view of the sentry, like you do before an All Blacks match, it will take his mind off Brush'. As you might imagine, they were as good as their word; as I went past puffing my cigar, with Terence beside me, they put the wind up me.

The time of their escape was chosen after careful observation of sentry changes and the comings and goings of the German security and administrative staffs.

We decided not to chance the outer gate, but to turn left into the German soldiers' quarters and thence round to a small corn field within the outer perimeter of wire, and it appeared [we] could find dead ground there to scale the single fence. We carried electric light bulbs, some flex and a coil of electric cable. The sentry looked at our passes and he and Terence exchanged 'Guten Morgens' and we were into the 'no man's land' between the two rows of wire, but outside the big double one; it now depended on the electrical equipment. We walked into the German Guard Company's barracks, there were a good many off duty soldiers about, but they took no notice of us until we reached the penultimate hut where several of them eyed us with interest. Terence put up his great act, he pushed past them, switched on the light at the door, 'Ach so! All well here?' sez Terence. 'Everything in order' answered the soldiers. In the meantime I gazed at the overhead cable where it entered the hut, and then joined in the 'So's'. You can go quite a long way in Germany with a 'So' spelt with a 'z'.

We hurried to the next hut which was unoccupied and then round the corner, there on the other side of the wire fence was a nosey holiday maker, gazing into the camp. Fortunately he was only strolling, the two electricians were on 'time and a half' and we reached the corner of the little cornfield a long way ahead of him. Once round the corner we flung ourselves into the three foot high

corn and hid until the coast was clear and we had got our breath.
Cautious reconnaissance seemed to reassure us that we were in
dead ground from the sentry towers, which proved to be so, as we
painfully climbed the barbed wire fence. We were free.

The process of getting outside a prisoner of war camp was only the first phase to an escape, as once a prisoner was out and away, they essentially became a fugitive. The main requirement for anybody while on the run was food; while prisoners would likely have a small supply of food on their person when escaping, or small amounts of money to buy supplies, this would soon run out and stealing or begging was the most realistic alternative source. To get regular food in occupied territory one needed to make contact with Allied sympathisers, although to locate and identify the appropriate people was far from straightforward. Few escaped prisoners worked alone, however. Most had already relied on fellow prisoners to help them get out of the camp, but then sought out resistance networks or sympathisers to work their way to freedom.

To move through a country in any significant way much official paperwork was required, which an authority figure might request to see at any time. In the case of escaped prisoners, this was almost always forged beforehand while still in the camp. As was the case with Peter Brush, genuine examples of the various documents were stolen or temporarily borrowed in order to allow the prisoners to copy them accurately. The main bureaucratic requirement in Germany was the *Ausweis* (identity card), together with work and travel permits for foreign workers. For the *Ausweis* in particular, photographs were required of the bearer. Cameras were obtained in several camps, either through bribery or theft, while sometimes prisoners made clever use of photographs already in their possession which could be cut up appropriately. The greatest challenge was how to reproduce printed text without proper facilities. The only way to achieve this was to draw by hand using ink, but with meticulous care. One tiny mistake could ruin weeks of careful work. Official ink stamps were forged by using a cut potato or etched linoleum.

Once out of their camp, Peter Brush and Terence Prittie attempted to put as much distance as possible between themselves and Oflag V-B. They covered seven miles fast, taking reasonable precautions to avoid meeting anybody by keeping away from main roads. The countryside of Württemberg, with its wide tracts of agricultural land and large pine forests, afforded them considerable cover.

The distance to the Schaffhausen Salient was 70 miles. We reckoned we had covered 12 of them by 4pm that afternoon. It had been a hot, tiring march. We had avoided being seen by anyone except a few locals working in the root fields or amongst the hay and corn. Some of them waved and shouted a greeting. Our blue dyed dungarees which were old pyjama coats and trousers apparently passed muster as local or foreign workers moving from one site to another. Anyhow, we occasioned no suspicion and we avoided the village of Buchau. In doing so we had to cross a quaking bog which was reminiscent to both of us of shooting snipe in Ireland, but when we got out of it we were absolutely exhausted, dripping with sweat and were thankful to get into thick cover where we lay up and went sound asleep for several hours, something we badly needed after the physical and mental strain of the day which we had just experienced.

We now had to change our tactics completely; for the first 12 miles which we had covered we had had to rely on speed to get us out of the immediate area of Biberach to avoid the close search which was obviously following us. Once after dark we intended to avoid all human contact as far as was possible between where we were now and the Schaffhausen Salient. At 9am we were awake, the sweat had dried on us, we were reasonably comfortable, our bellies were full of chocolate sludge. Our chief haversack ration for the four days was chocolate sludge made of Red Cross milk chocolate and oatmeal mixed into a form of cake. Fortunately, we also had some oatmeal without chocolate because the chocolate began to get a bit sickening on the second and third day. However our bellies were full, there was plenty of water in a stream nearby.

The two officers carried with them some rudimentary escape equipment.

We had a home-made compass with a magnetised needle and it was set in the top of a cigarette tin. It was reasonably accurate, pointed to the corner of a wood two miles due west which was the line we wanted to take. Then an industrious farmer arrived in a field a few yards away from us and started to turn his hay. The blighter went on working until half past ten when he shouldered his fork and went singing back home. About half past ten we were able to start on our long night march which we hoped would put us some 17 miles as the crow flies from Biberach. By 3.30am we were successful. In the 16 hours since we got out of camp, I think we covered 25 miles but only 17 in the direction which we wanted to go, due west for Schaffhausen. However, we were pleased at what we had achieved, we had avoided giving suspicion or giving ourselves away to anyone and we found a wood where we were able to lie up until 6am.

One of the problems faced by a fugitive was a reliance on the weather. So far the two men had been fortunate in that regard, but that was about to change for the worse.

There was a barn full of hay about 300 yards from where we were lying up and at 8pm that night rain started to fall steadily so we made a cautious entry into the barn, climbed right up to the top of the hay and hoped that by 11 when real darkness occurred that the rain would have ceased. Instead of ceasing it absolutely poured hour after hour with the lightning just overhead. We seemed to be in the vortex of a really good south-German thunderstorm. I think the Germans call it 'donner wetter und blitzen'. *We certainly had* 'donner wetter und blitzen' *all round us that night.*

Choosing the right time of year was crucial for a successful escape. Spending most of one's time outdoors in the middle of winter risked serious exposure and frostbite, while snow would reveal tracks if a prisoner was been hunted. Similarly, the spring and autumnal weather of eastern Europe would likely mean considerable mud in the countryside, meaning that any escaper could never stay clean and would have to attempt to pass as a vagrant, which limited the possibility of assistance from others and made the chances of being picked up by the local police much more likely. The summer months were therefore the best time of all to try to escape. This time of year also allowed for a greater chance of picking up food en route from the fields, gardens or orchards.

With no sign of the rain letting up, Brush and Prittie decided to stay the night in their barn and try for a double-length march the following evening. Despite a good start they ran into trouble when they encountered marshland, which slowed their progress considerably.

However, some time before dawn we did get out of the marshes, we got across the river and we got up on a ridge where we could see over to Lake Constance. The Bodensee of Germany and the Lake Constance of Switzerland, a wonderful sight in the dawn and we now had put 35 miles between us and Biberach and had something of the same distance to make to reach our goal in Switzerland. We were about half way and were well pleased with our night's work. We slept the next day in a very thick clump of thorn bushes and raspberry canes. The only danger was from school children who came to pick raspberries and were rather too close to us for comfort because there would be no doubt they'd have run and given us away if they'd come on us. During that day in the raspberry canes we made the decision which was to be fateful for us, that we would no longer follow the tracks and take the extreme precautions which we had taken to date, which avoided coming in contact with any living soul, but that we would use metalled roads and trust to our own alertness to get into a ditch or across a hedge if we bumped into anyone either on foot or on a bicycle or in a vehicle. We thought that the 20-odd miles in front of us now should be covered on better roads and that we should make the speed necessary to get near the frontier, because then we were all set to crawl the last few miles, if necessary.

Any escaped prisoner of war would be anxious of being noticed or questioned at any moment. Inquisitive farmers or townsfolk might be keen to court favour with the local authorities by reporting fugitives, while fanatically keen *Hitlerjugend* (Hitler Youth) formed a wide network of keen eyes. There were also problems associated with being helped by local civilians, as the punishment for the civilian if accused as a sympathiser could be very serious. They would be tried by a military court who had likely already decided on their guilt, with a probable sentence of either long-term imprisonment or immediate execution. There was also considerable danger for the escaper if recaptured, since if his claim to be an escaped prisoner wasn't believed, he might be accused of spying and simply shot without a proper trial. Escaped prisoners would likely have no real identity information to present to their captors, so their fate really depended on the attitude and compassion of those who arrested them. As far as Brush and Prittie were concerned, using roads meant that they were now more likely to encounter people.

The following day, members of the German Army arrived to escort the prisoners back to captivity.

Just what you'd expect in any army, a very tough corporal and two private soldiers. They marched us off to Pfullendorf Station where we caught a wonderful little train which puffed through Wurtemburg down in the direction of Radolfzell on the shores of Lake Constance. The corporal eyed us with great suspicion and was obviously very much on his toes to shoot us if we made any attempt to escape again. When we got into the carriage we sat side by side with one soldier on one side of us and one soldier on the other side of us and the corporal sitting opposite us. He said quite a long sentence in German. I listened to it, but to confirm it I said to Terence 'What did he say?' Terence said 'Oh, I don't know, something about shooting us if we tried to escape.' I said, 'Terence, I don't think he did. I think what he said was – he addressed himself to you as the younger and more mobile element of us two and he said 'Do you understand if you try to escape, I will shoot your comrade.'

The two men would suffer 28 days of solitary confinement, yet had survived to attempt escape again another day.

British military intelligence attempted to assist servicemen in captivity as best they could, both in terms of preparing them for the experience beforehand as well as offering assistance while they were prisoners of war. This was done through the work of MI9, the war office department with responsibility for this area. MI9 was set up in the final days of 1939, headed by Major Norman Crockatt and based in a room of the Metropole Hotel on Northumberland Avenue in London. Its main objectives were:

a) To facilitate escapes of British prisoners of war, thereby getting back service personnel and containing additional enemy manpower on guard duties.
b) To facilitate the return to the United Kingdom of those who succeeded in evading capture in enemy occupied territory.
c) To collect and distribute information.
d) To assist in the denial of information to the enemy.
e) To maintain morale of British prisoners of war in enemy prison camps.

An intelligence school was set up in Highgate where intelligence officers from all three services could be briefed on techniques for escape and evasion which they could then pass on to their individual units. These lectures developed in usefulness as the war progressed and as advice from newly repatriated and escaped prisoners was received. The idea was that once certain officers were in enemy hands, MI9 would be able to make contact with them via a pre-arranged code, included in letters sent via the prisoner of war's family. Only the most level-headed and sober officers were chosen, with the RAF as the priority service since they were most likely to fall into enemy hands if shot down. Prisoners could then request, in code, for particular escape aids to be sent to them, such as maps, money and clothing. Prisoners would then need to make efforts to ensure that when their illicit parcels arrived they were received intact, without the German authorities inspecting them too closely. There was plenty of scope to achieve this, since bribery of guards was widespread and parcel sorting offices in the camps were often staffed by prisoners themselves, under supervision.

MI9 was successful in establishing coded communication with every Oflag in Germany within seven months of the Dunkirk evacuation. During 1941–1942, they dispatched 1,642 parcels containing escape equipment, together with 5,173 ordinary parcels intended to provide cover for the 'special' ones by getting the German handlers used to their appearance. The parcels were addressed from fictitious senders such as the Licensed Victuallers Sports Association, the Prisoners' Leisure Hours Fund or the Welsh Provident Society. While in some cases the International Committee of the Red Cross acted as courier for the MI9 parcels, which might mean that they would be delivered in a box bearing the Red Cross symbol, MI9 were careful not to endanger the sanctity of the Red Cross food parcel. If the Germans realised that Red Cross parcels included forbidden items, they would likely forbid the prisoners from receiving the supplementary food. The ICRC itself gave an undertaking that they would never knowingly enclose escape equipment in their parcels.

Any escape tools or equipment were cleverly concealed, with instructions on how to locate them having been sent beforehand in coded letters. Hacksaw blades, screwdrivers and wire cutters were sent, hidden within a cricket bat handle perhaps, or depending on their size even in toothbrushes or combs. Suspecting that some parcels were contravening the regulations, the Germans started to x-ray incoming parcels in order to spot illicit items. Some items remained effectively hidden within specially constructed metal tins, perhaps filled with condensed milk, which would show up as blobs on the x-ray. Maps or money were especially easy to hide by being sealed within the outer and inner wrapper of such a tin. MI9 were unable to effectively provide forged documents, despite a few early attempts to do so, since the formats changed on a regular basis and the requirement for particular dates and names made it a tricky business.

Communication between home and the prisoners by letter or parcel was an incredibly slow process, so for the transmission of vital information, greater importance was placed on wireless receivers. Such equipment was forbidden in prisoner of war camps, but some captives (particularly airmen who might possess technical knowledge of wireless technology) were able to build their own crude sets from stolen materials, while others were smuggled into the camp in parcels. It was not long until almost every camp had a hidden receiver of some sort. The BBC's powerful transmitters could reach anywhere in the world and the opportunities for communication were therefore extensive. A weekly broadcast on Wednesday evenings made by a forces padre would sometimes contain coded information; if the broadcaster began his talk with 'Good evening, forces', it would alert the listeners that the talk would contain a secret message to be deciphered.

While the work of MI9 mainly benefitted those prisoners who were still inside camps by helping them to escape, they also provided limited assistance for the escaped prisoner on the run. Escape lines were set up in Belgium, France and the Netherlands, which helped fugitives to reach safety either in neutral countries such as Spain or Switzerland, or via ship back to Britain. However, this only really benefitted those who were evading capture in occupied territories. In the German homeland itself, where most of the main prisoner of war camps were generally located, escapers would receive little external assistance. Only those fugitives who could get near the coast or the border with Switzerland had any real chance for freedom. The location of certain camps was therefore chosen deliberately to make escaping as difficult as possible, with one of the most famous examples being Stalag Luft III, located in Lower Silesia. It was from here that two of the most famous escapes of the war were undertaken.

6 | Stalag Luft III

Escape is exceedingly difficult, as the Luftwaffe intended it should be when building the camp

Stalag Luft III was described by one of its prisoners, with an undoubted degree of sarcasm, as 'the wonderful new camp built especially for the RAF'. Constructed and run by the Luftwaffe, it was first occupied by Allied prisoners of war in April 1942. What began as a relatively small enclosure of two compounds grew considerably over time, with prisoner numbers also rising from a few hundred at first to over 10,000 at its peak. By the end of the war, the six compounds were occupied largely by American prisoners, yet for much of its time throughout the war the camp population included a very significant British contingent. The vast majority of prisoners held there were officers, despite the camp's designation as a Stalag rather than an Oflag; its naming convention reflected the camp's status as a Luftwaffe-run prison.

The camp was located in the German province of Lower Silesia, some 90 miles south-east of Berlin. The nearest large town was Sagan, with a population of around 25,000, and the area in which the camp was located had been carefully chosen for its remoteness from any battle zones as well as being a considerable distance from any friendly or neutral borders. Sagan was an important railway junction, which made the transport of prisoners much easier than might otherwise have been the case. In the event, this transport hub would also prove handy to those prisoners of war who managed to escape from the confines of the camp. The camp itself was bordered by forests of pine trees, while the very sandy nature of the ground meant that tunnelling was particularly difficult and any evidence of displaced soil quite noticeable.

Stalag Luft III was well designed and initially based around four areas: the German barracks and buildings of the *Kommandantur*; the *Vorlager*, containing facilities such as the Red Cross parcel store, a dentist, theatre and chapel, as well as the 'cooler' cells for solitary confinement; the East Compound, with eight barracks for officers; and the Centre Compound, with twelve barracks for NCOs. The two compounds were designed to collectively hold 2,500 prisoners and each included facilities such as cookhouses, fire pools and small sports fields. Every single-storey barrack was split internally into different rooms, each with multiple double bunk beds. Some rooms were set aside as recreation space or a library/reading room, while every barrack had large windows which were covered by shutters at night. Each room usually had a small stove and in each compound a barrack was designated for use as a theatre or gymnasium. The Centre Compound theatre was so well designed that it could boast a large stage and even an orchestra pit.

Flying Officer Oliver Philpot arrived at Stalag Luft III on 29 April 1942, having been shot down in December over the North Sea off Norway, while attacking a German naval convoy. After spending two days at sea in their escape dinghy, he and his crew were picked up by a German naval vessel and he then spent a few months in various prisoner of war transit camps before being transferred to Sagan. On arrival, he began to make notes on the conditions and facilities he found there. Although Stalag Luft III was a new, carefully designed camp, certain of its facilities actually left a lot to be desired.

A hutted camp, rectangular barbed wire compounds surrounded by a pine forest. Eight men to a room. For first 18 months (approximately), from 700 to 800 men to 6 cold water taps (excluding cookhouse ones). All washing, personal and clothes, all water for rooms, from these six taps. No water system for lavatories; excreta pumped into carts and taken away. Camp admitted by Hauptmann Kiesslich in conversation with Wing Commander M F D Williams DSC to be 'primitive and filthy'. The East Compound, where we were, was built slowly and carefully and not too big from the Luftwaffe viewpoint (992 paces round the inside). It is hence practically escape-proof. Large danger strip, well-placed raised sentry boxes, sentries in boxes with tommy guns always on shoulders, good perimeter lights and swivelling searchlights, a double gate before one can get out of the camp.

Escape activity in summer 1942 [was] fast and furious. People climbing on to carts and wagons, men disguised as Germans, men doing hard work on tunnels (about 45 to 60, in all, that season). But all to no avail, except small self-sealing tunnel by Lamont, Best and another. [They] were in this for 33 hours. Also, epic wire-cutting feat in broad daylight, with most elaborate diversions, by Toft and Nicholls. But all five recaptured.

Entertainments run by Wing Commander Larkin AFC. These of high standard but 'theatre' space terribly cramped. Sports – football, cricket – on small pitch provided. Small fire-water pond about 25 feet square used as swimming pool. Attitude of Luftwaffe at first 'the big hand' to their 'brothers of the air', later distinctly stiffer due to us not playing with them regarding not escaping or anything else. Camp watched from inside by German Luftwaffe 'ferrets' in overalls who crawl about looking for tunnels or eavesdrop at windows. Wing Commander Bader DSO DFC [was] a continual thorn in sides of Germans and removed to an Army camp.

The capture of ever-increasing numbers of Allied airmen meant that Stalag Luft III and other Luftwaffe camps were beginning to fill rapidly, encouraging the Germans to begin work on building a new compound to the west of the *Kommandantur* in the autumn of 1942. Coming into use at the end of March 1943, this became known as North Compound and was larger than the other two compounds combined, containing 15 barrack huts, a cookhouse, a theatre and an unusually large playing field. The entire compound was designed to hold an additional 1,200 men. As 1943 began and the camp increased in size, the prisoners' initial appetite to escape was beginning to fade. Oliver Philpot was the escape coordinator for his particular hut in the East Compound.

[The East Compound] produces a deadening effect on many minds somehow – mine amongst them. Possibly it is because of its rectangular pattern, and almost geometrical layout. Some new tunnels tried but after failure of most of last summer's terrific escape efforts, enthusiasm quite naturally not exactly at fever pitch. Most people settling down to some solid work (the education system is excellent) and vigorous sport or exercise. The other compounds are bigger and North, especially, more difficult for the Germans to control. From the new North compound a party of about 30 were marched out by a bogus guard – they were ostensibly going to have a shower (I think) – and faded into the woods. But a big 'flap' and all captured. Again demonstrating [the] disadvantage of a big break, the Germans are stirred up as wasps by a stick being put into their nest.

Escape is exceedingly difficult as the Luftwaffe intended it should be when building the camp. I do not think anyone had got home direct from Sagan, and no one had succeeded in making a local break from the East Compound (where I was) for over a year. Wire schemes are suicidal and orthodox tunnels are found (somewhere between 45 and 60 of them in summer 1943) since the Germans have an uncanny knack of finding traps situated under our barrack room blocks. There are two gates and an ever-changing pass system. I mention all this to answer the question, 'Well, why don't more people escape from Sagan?' The only method from the East Compound is, I think, something entirely new and original.

As we shall see, he could not have been more correct. The summer months of 1943 saw a greater deal of involvement by the Gestapo in the running of Stalag Luft III, which Philpot noted as 'a disturbing feature of camp'.

Gestapo were first interested because of bribery cases. We adopted a non-speaking policy to all Germans and first of all told them we resented having anything to do with civil police as we were military prisoners of war, and as long as they 'played ball' with the Gestapo we regarded them as the lowest of the low. Now Gestapo have faded into background again. In September or October [we] had visit from German Foreign Office, a Herr Reindhart. Almost immediate result was issue (quite unexpected) of many much-needed greatcoats from Booty Store. Lager-officer Schultz, when asked by the Compound Adjutant Squadron Leader McDonnell why this surprising event had taken place, said 'Perhaps they have seen the light.'

A sad footnote to life in Stalag Luft III reveals how life in captivity could impact on the mental health of the prisoners of war, while serving as a reminder of the harsh Nazi regime.

An unpleasant thing [this] summer was shooting of Lieutenant Kiddell. This officer was clearly unbalanced, the British authorities had strenuously applied for his removal to a home, the Germans had said it was a sham and then taken no action. Kiddell quietly left the camp sick-bay one night and was later, when near the wire, killed by a sentry. He was wearing pyjamas.

Despite the impression of inactivity on the escape front, two fellow prisoners from Philpot's barracks had approached him in June 1943 to discuss the possibility of carrying out an escape plan that they had formulated. The two men, 2nd Lieutenant Michael Codner and Flight Lieutenant Eric Williams, had first met in Oflag XXI-B at Schubin, where they had successfully escaped through a tunnel only to be swiftly recaptured. They were now determined to try their luck again at Stalag Luft III, and received Philpot's support as a third collaborator. Codner's presence in the camp was somewhat unusual, since he was a Royal Artillery officer as opposed to an airman, but it is likely that his reputation as an escaper had led to his transfer there along with Williams. Their plan involved taking advantage of the exercise facilities in East Compound, which were located conveniently near to the edge of the camp.

> *A hollow vaulting horse, light but strong, was constructed by Wing Commander Maw DFC out of some stolen pieces of wood and the three-ply from Canadian Red Cross boxes. This was carried by four men and used to be placed quite openly close to the wire. Vaulting then took place and when finished the horse was taken back to the canteen building, where it was housed. The horse itself was in fact quite a good athletic horse and the Germans accepted it as such. The real object was to have the horse to conceal the entrance to a tunnel, the advantages being twofold: firstly, it was near the wire, secondly, the entrance of the tunnel was thus in a highly original spot – out in the open flat ground in full view of everybody, British and German alike, except that there was nothing to see, since after work was completed the hole was boarded over and carefully covered with sand to resemble the adjacent surface. It could be, and was frequently, walked over.*

The plan began to be put into operation on 8 July 1943.

> *The method of work was as follows: when the horse was taken out for a vaulting session one of us would be inside in its belly. This*

person would then open up the trap, work at the tunnel, fill with sand 12 bags (consisting of cut-off trouser legs below the knee) and hang these bags inside the horse. He would then close the trap, taking a long time to cover it over carefully, squeeze himself into one end of the horse, and be carried off.

The problem remained as to how they would dispose of the soil, although once again ingenuity saved the day. The three officers were aided by their fellow prisoners, comrades who assisted them selflessly in the knowledge that they would not be able to join in the escape themselves.

Disposal of the sand was the usual nightmare difficulty and in all about ten methods were used, two of which were found by the Germans who felt there was something going on but they didn't know what. We settled down to using chiefly the canteen roof and the space under the barber's shop in the canteen. The scheme began on July 8th and was, of course, very slow, due to the limited amount of sand which could be removed at any one time. Codner and Williams did the first 40 feet alone, going down in turns, working entirely naked, and 'side stroking' the sand down the tunnel to the entrance. Later we had an improved system with a basin and string. Two people went down, one at the face and one at the entrance, and the latter pulled down basins of sand from the former. 36 bags of sand would be produced in this way and left down there. On each of the next three occasions one man would come out and collect 12 bags. The work was tiring and the air was poor.

All the vaulting took place in full view of a guard in a raised box nearby who used to laugh at some of the less commendable efforts at vaulting. Previously, also, it had always been the custom to work on escape operations only when the 'ferrets' or German security soldiers were out of the camp. Now, however, they are always in the camp, patrolling anywhere they fancy in numbers varying from one to seven at a time. So to get anything done at all caution had to be thrown to the winds and we worked with them in the camp. Throughout we had quite extraordinary luck in evading detection. One day 'Charlie', the German security Unteroffizier, walked up to within six feet of the horse when operations were proceeding and suggested that the vaulters would find it easier if they had a springboard. They agreed.

The whole scheme was only made possible by a volunteer band of extremely unselfish helpers who were called on to come and vault time and time again, and who knew they never had any chance of escaping themselves. Members of the Escape Committee were amongst those who went out of their way not only to give general help but came and vaulted themselves.

The three men had already prepared their cover stories for once they were out of the camp and on the run, and had in readiness their civilian clothing and fake identity papers. Codner and Williams would travel together, posing as French workers; the former could speak excellent French and would help to cover for Williams. It was agreed that Philpot would make his own separate way to freedom by posing as a Norwegian salesman named Jörgensen. Eric Williams later described their preparations in his own account of the Wooden Horse escape.

I was dressed in a beret made from a German blanket, an Imperial Airways raincoat, a black converted Marine's uniform and black shoes. I carried a small leather attaché case in which I had my escape food, shaving kit and a black roll-collar sweater for my role as a Swedish sailor. For the actual break I wore woollen combinations dyed black, with a black hood over my head. My jacket and raincoat were in a long sausage-shaped bag, also black. I was clad in long woollen underwear, but found this insufficient when sleeping out at night. My papers consisted of: Vorläufiger Ausweis; Arbeitskarte [job card]; police permission to travel; reason for travel supplied by firm of Reichsbauant; a doubtful Swedish sailor's pass; 150 Reichsmarks; a photograph of a stunning girl inscribed 'A mon cher marcel – Jeanne'; and two letters written in French to myself, 'Marcel Levasseur'.

The date for the escape attempt was decided upon as 29 October.

We had arranged to break the tunnel at 6pm in order to catch the Frankfurt train, which departs at 7pm. As we still had several feet to dig, Codner went down at 12.30pm and started to dig, filling in the tunnel behind him as he went forward. After the 4.30pm roll call I went down and crawled up the tunnel to send the loose sand back to Philpot, who remained in the vertical shaft to put the sand into bags to be taken back with the vaulting horse. I found the tunnel thick with steam and very hot, but Codner cheerful but extremely dirty. After the trap at the end of the tunnel had been closed Philpot crawled up to about halfway and moved forward, dispersing the sand I sent back over the face of the tunnel. We all worked without ceasing until 6.05pm when we emerged.

The tunnel's final length was almost 100 feet with its exit located in the open, about 15 to 18 feet beyond the wire. The three men started to creep out of the tunnel exit one by one, each carrying their items of kit; Codner first, Williams second and Philpot last. Luckily, due to some oversight, the German guards patrolling on foot outside the perimeter of the camp had not yet appeared and the sentry-box guards failed to spot the prisoners emerging. Each man was dressed in a mask and dyed black suit to protect their civilian outfits, with their parcels of supplies for the journey ahead being similarly camouflaged so as not to be seen in the searchlights. Reaching the nearby woods where they wished each other good luck, Philpot would then travel alone while Williams and Codner were to follow their own route. The two separate parties initially both headed to Sagan railway station.

Codner bought two tickets to Frankfurt. In the booking hall of the station I came face to face with the German doctor who had been treating me in the hospital only two days before. Fortunately I had cut off my rather heavy moustache and I was not recognised. The train journey was uneventful. The train was extremely crowded and perfectly dark. We stood in the corridor. We arrived at Frankfurt at 8.50pm and tried to get a room at four hotels. These were all full, so we walked out of the town and spent the night in a drain. It was dry and sheltered, but extremely cold. We had intended to spend all our nights under cover and had not taken enough warm clothing. We came out before dawn.

By now Philpot had embarked on his separate escape route, while Williams and Codner caught a further train, this time to Küstrin.

The train was very crowded and once again we had to stand. The first carriage we entered was full of Russian prisoners of war. We were turned out by the German guard. Fortunately the Germans are very used to incompetent foreigners and one has only to say 'Ich bin Ausländer' *['I am a foreigner'] and look helpless.*

Arriving at the Baltic Sea port of Stettin, the two men began their attempts to locate a ship that might take them to neutral Sweden. What little money they possessed allowed them to book hotel rooms, but only for two nights at a time. The local police would have to be notified of a longer stay, and the fugitives needed to maintain their cover as itinerant workers. To remain inconspicuous they visited the local cinema, watching the same film four times in a row while failing to understand a word of it. After dark both men sought to make contact with French dock workers in the hope of contacting a ship destined for Sweden, yet this had to be done subtly in case the authorities were alerted.

> *We once more started our rounds of the cafés. During this we consumed large quantities of German beer, which is very inferior in quality and seems to contain absolutely no alcohol. At one café we met a Frenchman who was very anxious to help us, but was so furtive in his manner and so obviously a conspirator that he was rather a liability than an asset. He took us to another café where he sat us down at a table and told the waitress in a loud voice that we were Swedes and that if any more Swedes came in they were to be shown to our table. He then walked out and a German woman came across to us and started to talk in Swedish. I immediately mumbled something and walked out, while Codner tried to explain that I was Swedish and he was French. It was a nasty moment.*

Finally, some progress was made. On their fifth day as fugitives, they sneaked into a labour camp and met with a French prisoner of war, Andre Daix, who had been supplying information to agents in Denmark. He in turn put them in contact with somebody who was able to get them on board the SS *I.C. Jacobson*, which was due to sail for Oslo. On 11 November, the ship arrived at its final destination and the two fugitives were put ashore with the Swedish pilot at 5pm. There were German passengers aboard the ship which made the whole operation extremely dangerous, as the possibility existed that the two escaped prisoners might still be identified at any moment, but they were now finally in neutral territory. The two men were taken to the local police station where they enjoyed a bath and meal despite having to spend a night in the cells, while the following day they were taken to Gothenburg, where the British Consul met and fed them before they were forwarded to Stockholm and safety.

In Stockholm they were soon reunited with Oliver Philpot, who had arrived separately in the city a week before, on 4 November.

His entire escape had taken fewer than 5 days, and had involved taking a series of trains from Sagan to Danzig, where he managed to smuggle himself onto a Swedish ship called the *Aralizz*. Williams, Codner and Philpot could claim to be the only three prisoners of war to have successfully escaped from Stalag Luft III's East Compound and make their way to freedom, thereby proving that such a feat was indeed possible. However, an even more audacious escape attempt from the camp was to follow in due course.

Back at Sagan, living space was at a premium. The Italian surrender on 3 September 1943 resulted in many thousands of Allied prisoners of war being transported to new accommodation in Germany, and fortuitously the new South Compound at Stalag Luft III, which opened for business on 8 September, allowed an additional 1,175 men to be accommodated. By the end of the year, Stalag Luft III was filled to capacity. The Germans' intention was to house American prisoners separately to the British and by the end of the war this was largely the case, with all but 600 out of a total of 10,000 prisoners of war being resident in their designated areas of the camp – mainly the South Compound and, after its construction in April 1944, the West Compound, which proved to be the largest of all. Around 1,200 prisoners, mainly British and Commonwealth, had already been sent to a satellite camp located at Belaria, about 3 miles to the west on a hill overlooking Sagan, in January 1944.

It is tempting to think that the daring nature of the 'Wooden Horse' escape was a direct inspiration for the next significant break-out from Stalag Luft III, which occurred just over five months later, in March 1944. This time, the attempt would be made from North Compound. The mass nature of the escape and the harsh reprisals which followed would earn its reputation as 'the Great Escape'. The mastermind behind the plan was Squadron Leader Roger Bushell, a South African-born officer who had been flying with No 92 Squadron RAF when he was shot down over the French coast on 23

May 1940. It was the Squadron's first ever operational engagement with enemy aircraft.

As soon as the battle started about four or five of them fell on me and oh boy did I start dodging. My first I got with a full deflection shot from underneath. He went down in a long glide with his port engine pouring smoke, and I went into a spin as two others were firing at me from my aft quarter... I then saw a Messerschmitt below me trying to fire up at me so I went head on at him and he came head on at me. We were both firing and everything was red flashes. I killed the pilot because suddenly he pulled right up at me and missed me by inches. I went over the top of him and as I turned saw him rear right up in a stall and go down with his engine smoking...

My engine was shot up and I force landed and it burst into flames. I got out with extreme celerity and except for a bump on the nose which didn't even break it I was untouched. I sat by my machine and had a cigarette and watched it burn and then to my rage and astonishment a German motorbike came round the corner and I was taken prisoner. I thought of course that I was well behind our lines.

It was the duty of all officer prisoners of war to attempt to escape, and Bushell clearly considered this his priority. He slipped from his German escorts while on an excursion away from his first camp and almost reached the Swiss border in May 1941 before being spotted by an observant frontier guard. Then, while being transferred by train to a new camp in October 1941, he and the Czech pilot Jaroslav Zafouk jumped from their carriage and managed to escape to occupied Prague, where they made contact with the Czechoslovakian resistance. They hid in the city for eight months but, following the assassination of *SS-Obergruppenführer* Reinhard Heydrich in May 1942, security was tightened up and both Bushell and Zafouk were apprehended by the authorities. Both officers received rough interrogations by the Gestapo before Roger was transferred to what would be his final prisoner of war camp, Stalag Luft III, in October 1942. It was from here that he managed to get a letter back to his parents.

Here I am again! I escaped last October, was hidden in Prague during the intervening period, and was unfortunately recaptured last month. That explains everything I think. Further details I will tell you after the war. You will I know have had a very anxious and trying time but I also know that you would not have expected me, in the circumstances, to have done anything other than I did and we will therefore leave it at that. I am quite OK and very well so you have nothing to worry about. This is a Luftwaffe camp, with old friends from Dulag of both nationalities here, so I am in excellent hands. At the moment I am in the 'cooler' doing my stretch for my escape... Am naturally bitterly disappointed at having been caught again but my spirits are sky high and you need have no fear that this life has got me down yet and that it ever will, please God.

Soon appointed as leader of the camp's Escape Committee under the moniker of 'Big X', Roger Bushell ensured that the business of escaping was treated as a serious endeavour, marshalling resources in a way that many other camps failed to achieve. This rejection of 'amateurish' attempts and decision to concentrate on a detailed, long-term escape strategy was characterised by the choice to dig multiple escape tunnels, the logic being that if one tunnel was discovered by the Germans, they would not necessarily expect others to exist. Sure enough, one of the tunnels (nicknamed 'Tom') was identified and dynamited by the guards, while another ('Dick') was abandoned after it was discovered that the Germans intended to expand the camp's perimeter far beyond the intended exit point. 'Dick' was thenceforth used to store soil and materials while the prisoners concentrated on digging the third tunnel, nicknamed 'Harry'. This began in hut 104, its entrance hidden under a stove, descended over 8 metres and then ran underground for just over

100 metres before emerging at the beginning of woodland to the north of the camp.

The break-out via tunnel 'Harry' on the night of 24–25 March 1944 resulted in the escape of 76 prisoners of war, including Bushell himself. In total, 220 prisoners were lined up in readiness to escape, but the guards spotted the 77th man emerging from the tunnel and the alarms were sounded, bringing an end to the venture. Over the next few weeks, 73 prisoners were recaptured including Roger Bushell and his escape partner Bernard Scheidhauer, who were both apprehended at Saarbrucken railway station.

On the personal orders of Adolf Hitler and in direct breach of the Geneva Conventions, 50 of the escapees were executed as an example and Roger Bushell was included among their number. In spite of the failure of the Great Escape to result in many of its participants reaching safety, it could be argued that the escape occasioned some larger, more long-lasting achievements. Major Keith Mountfort, a Major in the Parachute Regiment who was held captive in Stalag Luft III at the time of the escape, wrote to Bushell's parents after the war.

In his final briefing before the 24th March, Roger, with the senior British officer standing at his side, explained the objects of the operation. He said that apart from the value of getting some experienced officers back to England, one vital factor was to cause alarm and inconvenience throughout a large area of Germany. Another was to cause extra precautionary measures to be taken by the Germans and necessitate extra guards and the replacement of certain camp staff. All these were accomplished, including the eventual sacking of the Kommandant, *his second in command, the security officer and other officials.*

By the middle of 1944, the patience of the German authorities in putting up with regular escapes from prisoner of war camps had run out. The mass break-out from Stalag Luft III was the final straw. Printed leaflets began to be distributed to all in captivity, advising that 'the escape from prison camps is no longer a sport!' and warning that fugitives identified as escaped prisoners of war would be shot on sight. Himmler and the SS took over responsibility for preventing escape from prisoner of war camps and crucially were also responsible for recapturing escaped prisoners. Any recaptured prisoner would be unlikely to receive another opportunity to offend.

In the 6 months from April to November 1944, largely as a result of the Allied campaign in north-west Europe, the population of Stalag Luft III doubled from just over 5,000 to more than 10,000. Over-crowding became a huge problem. Tents were introduced to cope with the need for additional sleeping space, while food rations became smaller and disease and sickness more common as living conditions deteriorated. To make matters even worse, the news of the Russian advances to the east made everyone nervous. Some prisoners feared that they would be used as hostages by the Germans, while others expected forced marches away from the combat zones. By mid January 1945, it was common knowledge in the camp that the Russian advances were growing ever closer. For the first time in four and a half months, the camp's senior officers put their men on full rations in order to build up their health and prepare them for any eventuality. The likelihood was that they would all be marched away to the west, and many prisoners made individual efforts to regain their fitness in readiness for the exertions to come, packing their few belongings so that they would be ready to move out at short notice.

About 7pm on the evening of 27 January, the order was given to evacuate Stalag Luft III as news was received that the Russians had reached the River Oder. Throughout the night and early the next day each compound was emptied of prisoners, the hastiness of the operation resulting in many supplies being left behind, including perhaps as many as 55,000 Red Cross food parcels, 1 million books and over 2.5 million cigarettes. About 500 prisoners were too sick to be moved and would be transported away by train a week or so later, but the thousands of other Allied prisoners assembled into several columns and began their long march westwards. Everybody suffered, with the wintry weather conditions making the roads treacherous and the prisoners' extreme hunger accentuating the hardship. The men from South Compound alone marched for 34 and a half miles in the first 27 hours, with only one 4-hour stop. Few prisoners took the opportunity to escape, since the blizzard conditions they endured suggested that keeping together was the wisest decision. In addition, a general order had been transmitted by the BBC and picked up by camp wireless sets that prisoners of war were to stay together for safety and ease of identification.

Many of Stalag Luft III's American prisoners were destined for Stalag XIII-D outside Nuremberg and Stalag VII-A near Moosburg, while the British and Commonwealth prisoners largely ended up at Marlag-Milag Nord at Westertimke. Prisoners from East Compound and the Belaria satellite camp were transferred to Luckenwalde, near Berlin. All would be liberated in due course, although the thoughts of those servicemen who had survived those last few months of harsh living would no doubt have lingered on their comrades who were not so fortunate. The fate of the 50 prisoners executed as a reprisal to the Great Escape would in particular come to symbolise the harsh treatment practised by the Third Reich towards its prisoners of war.

7 | Colditz

Here are collected all the bright lads who have been trying to get home ever since they were caught

Located near Leipzig in eastern Germany, Colditz Castle perches on a rocky outcrop overlooking the River Mulde some 250 feet below. Originally dating from Renaissance times, the castle served many different purposes throughout its existence, becoming a mental hospital in the nineteenth century, then a sanatorium and, following the rise of the Nazis, was transformed into a political prison to house the regime's most 'undesirables'. Upon the outbreak of war, Colditz was formally designated as the prisoner of war camp Oflag IV-B. Even in peacetime it would have seemed like a threatening destination, yet the trappings of war had turned the castle into a cold, bleak prison. Its outer walls were seven feet thick, and the sheer drop on one side of the building limited the potential escape routes.

As an Oflag, the castle was intended for Allied officer prisoners and the first ones had arrived in November 1939. Initially, many different nationalities were imprisoned there and by the end of July 1941 there were over 500 officers in captivity, mainly Polish and French at this time, with only 50 men from Britain or its Commonwealth. The nationality mix of the inmates would change over time, however. In May 1943, the Wehrmacht High Command decreed that the castle would concentrate on housing British and American officers. By the end of July that year, there were some 228 British officers, accompanied by a few Free French, while the remainder of the prisoners consisted of a handful of Canadian, Australian, New Zealand, South African, Irish and Indian servicemen. When Colditz received its first 3 American officers in August 1944, the total prison population numbered 254.

Colditz was designated as a high-security *Sonderlager* prison and developed the reputation of being impossible to escape from. This status meant that Colditz was the location where particularly high-profile prisoners were most likely to be sent. These *Prominente* were largely relatives of important Allied leaders and politicians, and as such were considered useful to the Germans as potential hostages. They included Dawyck Haig (Lord Haig, and the son of the famous First World War field marshal), Lord Hopetoun (the son of the Viceroy of India), Lord Lascelles and Lord Elphinstone (both nephews of King George VI) and John Winant (son of the US Ambassador to Britain). One of the most significant of the *Prominente* was Giles Romilly, a civilian journalist captured in Norway who happened to be a nephew of Prime Minister Winston Churchill's wife, Clementine. Romilly's importance was reinforced by the issue of a specific order from Adolf Hitler himself, stating in no uncertain terms that the camp's Commandant and security officer would personally answer for any harm that befell Romilly with their heads. It is perhaps unsurprising that many of the *Prominente* took advantage of their special status; Romilly objected so much to the constant tramp of his guards' feet outside his cell that, following a visit from Red Cross inspectors, a red carpet was laid to muffle the noise. Another officer, Michael Alexander, managed to escape an execution order by claiming (falsely) to be a nephew of the British Field Marshal Harold Alexander.

After the war, other personalities were associated with having spent time in captivity in Colditz. Perhaps the most famous of these was British fighter pilot Douglas Bader, shot down over France in August 1941. Despite requiring two prosthetic legs to walk following a flying accident earlier in his life, Bader was involved in a number of escape attempts from prisoner of war camps and sought every opportunity to make things difficult for his German captors. It was perhaps inevitable that he was transferred to Colditz in August 1942, where he would remain until liberation. Other notable individuals imprisoned in the castle included David Stirling, founder of the elite Special Air Service (SAS), who arrived in August 1944, and Captain Charles Upham, the New Zealander who had been awarded the Victoria Cross for heroism shown during the Battle for Crete in May 1941. Following his liberation, Upham would receive a further distinction by being awarded a Bar to his VC for heroism shown during the Battle of El Alamein in July 1942. Another prisoner who would gain fame after the war was Airey Neave, the future Shadow Secretary of State for Northern Ireland, whose fate was to be assassinated by the Irish National Liberation Army in 1979.

Colditz's reputation was largely based on propaganda promulgated by the Germans, with *Reichsmarschall* Hermann Goering famously ordering that the castle should be 'escape-proof'. Yet this claim was proven to be inaccurate, as Colditz boasted at least 32 successful escape attempts from inside the castle throughout the war, of which 15 resulted in 'home runs'. Some have claimed even greater numbers by including escapes made from the grounds or outbuildings, or from nearby hospitals or while being transported elsewhere. In terms of *attempted* escapes, however, there were many hundreds being undertaken on a regular basis.

The importance of the castle as a high-security prison meant that it boasted a significant German garrison of around 200 guards. Additional civilian workers were based in the castle grounds and nearby, while the families of staff were located in designated quarters inside the walls. Having already served his country during the First

World War, German school teacher Reinhold Eggers was recalled to military service in 1939 and posted to work as a translator at Oflag IV-A in Hohnstein. In November the following year, he was transferred to IV-C at Colditz, to serve as a duty officer. He gained a good degree of respect from the prisoners, probably due to his calm, reasonable manner but also helped by the fact that he was one of the few English-speakers among the German guards. Eggers' steady, pragmatic conduct ultimately led to his promotion in February 1944 to security officer for the castle, but throughout his time at Colditz he maintained a daily register of notable happenings which included, of course, the numerous escape attempts. If we look at just one month's entries, in this case covering May 1941, we can see the regularity of attempted escapes from the castle.

8th: British Lieutenant Allan escapes hidden in a straw mattress. Reaches Vienna.

9th: Polish Lieutenants Chmiel and Surmanowicz caught in the attic of the Saalhaus. Both these Poles open their arrest cells, reach the attic of the cellarhaus and go down by a rope of 22 bed linen. Caught nearby.

14th: Polish Lieutenant Just escapes from a cell under the vaults. Caught in the Rhine.

29th: Canteen tunnel attempt. 11 British, 2 Poles caught.

31st: French Lieutenant Colin disappears. Time, route, disguise, unknown.

These are, of course, only the escape attempts that the Germans were able to successfully identify; there would have been many more of which they were never aware.

As a *Sonderlager*, Colditz became the location where particularly troublesome Allied officers would be held captive including, in particular, serial escapers.

Colditz was never designed as a prison, yet had been adapted to fulfil its new function. The German garrison were housed in the *Kommandantur*, a large outer court with only two exits, one leading through the main gate across a dry moat drawbridge and the other allowing access to a narrow road which led down to what was known as 'the park'. The prisoners' quarters were situated around an adjacent, inner courtyard, regularly patrolled by sentries. This part of the castle included areas such as the parcel office, chapel, canteen, theatre and prisoners' kitchen. Apart from the side adjacent to the *Kommandantur*, the prisoners' block was surrounded by steep drops on all sides, with small terraces regularly patrolled by guards. Barbed wire, machine gun posts and searchlights complemented the security of the castle building itself.

The Oflag suffered somewhat from its size; while being a very secure location well-suited for use as a prison, the lack of proper exercise facilities proved detrimental to the inmates. The nearby piece of land known as 'the park', located outside the main castle, was an attempt to address this problem. The opportunity to see something different from the inner walls of the castle meant that such trips were popular among the Allied officers. But there were other, more nefarious reasons for their keenness to exercise, since any reason to be outside the castle would heighten their chances for executing a successful escape. This was proven to be the case by the French Cavalry Officer Pierre Mairesse-Lebrun who, with assistance from a fellow prisoner, managed to catapult himself over the park's wire fence and run to cover before the guards' rifle fire could target him. Initially still dressed in his sports clothes, he managed to steal a bicycle and made his way to Switzerland and freedom. Such was the effect of this audacious daylight escape over the park fence in the minds of the prisoners that it would be emulated in September 1944 by British Lieutenant Michael Sinclair, nicknamed the 'Red Fox'. On that occasion, however, the escape attempt ended in disaster. Sinclair was fatally shot: the victim of the only confirmed fatality in the castle due to an escape attempt.

The camaraderie and shared determination to escape meant that life as a prisoner in Colditz was actually much better than that experienced in most other prisoner of war camps. Lieutenant Colonel 'Milts' Reid had been serving with the special reconnaisance GHQ Liaison Regiment in Greece when he was captured in April 1941. He spent time in a number of different prisoner of war camps until arriving at Colditz in September 1943. He soon wrote to his wife to tell her about his new home.

Arrived here safely 23rd and am well settled in. Trip took twelve hours and was for me very interesting as first time I've travelled alone with a tame obliging guard – in fact it was like an outing – six changes en route... I had only short distances to carry two suitcases, bedding-roll (round neck), haverbag and trug basket: books and stock cigs and food follow with my precious chair. I met a party of young USA aviators in train, interesting as they were new arrivals. Plenty old friends here from VI-B, all much more lively than cloister air of IX-A/H! Presume I'm sent here for stuff I may have written for fortune but the Germans don't give reasons: on balance camp greatly superior to any other in accommodation: two others in room 18' x 22', nice view, single beds, private cooking, hot water, separate dining room for mess of eight, plugs that pull, in fact a much higher standard than any I've ever had. Exercise facilities slightly worse than IX-A. (Bader, the legless airman, who is POW here has just interrupted me to ask if your photo is of my daughter!), on balance everything better except library which I shall miss but I'm MUCH more comfy than I've ever been...

Here are collected all the bright lads who have been trying to get home ever since they were caught and the Germans have taken steps to prevent it. I'm told in peacetime it's a 'loony bin'; from some stories I'm told it's not far from one now – you and GI would rock laughing if you could hear some of the accounts! [...] If people tell you this is a straflager *[punishment camp] don't take any imaginative flights of me in stocks because, I repeat, I'm better off than I've ever been.*

The prevalence of so many experienced escapers, coupled with officers who had been labelled as particularly opposed to the Nazi regime, meant that the atmosphere among the captives in Colditz was remarkably positive and morale was high. When prisoners were not thinking about escape, they were taking delight in taunting their German captors, as described by Flight Lieutenant Hedley Fowler.

The only method of retaliation by the prisoners of war is what is known as 'Boche Baiting', and is under the able direction of Wing Commander Bader RAF. This consists of annoying the Germans on all possible occasions, by refusing to understand German, by rigging 'booby traps', by writing pamphlets giving the truth about Germany, by demonstrating during roll calls, and in many other ways.

When not planning escapes, prisoners followed the usual pastime for those in wartime captivity of making their own entertainment. Sport was always popular and at Colditz largely undertaken in the nearby park. August 1941 saw the Polish prisoners organise their own 'Olympics' consisting of football, boxing, volleyball and chess contests. The British contingent ranked last. Theatrical entertainment was also always popular, and this was largely led by the British. Numerous revues, plays and pantomimes were performed to the great delight of their ready-made audience and a repertory system was introduced in which new productions were shown on a regular basis, sometimes as often as a new one every fortnight.

There was also illicit entertainment. Moonshine alcohol was brewed from the contents of Red Cross parcels by combining yeast, water, sugar and other ingredients in secret stills hidden throughout the castle. Prisoner Michael Farr, whose family back home ran Hawker's Gin, managed to make a sparkling wine which was dubbed 'Château Colditz'. Another forbidden pastime was listening to BBC broadcasts received via one of two secret radio sets hidden in the castle. Known as 'Arthur 1' and 'Arthur 2', one radio was discovered by the Germans early on, but the other would remain a secret throughout the war. The hiding places in the castle for items such as stills or radio sets were many and so effective that in several cases hidden objects were still being found in the castle some 50 years or so after the end of the war.

Every prisoner of war camp had weaknesses in its security and these would be exploited by the prisoners wherever possible to expedite an escape. In the case of Colditz castle, one of the easiest 'ways out' discovered early on had proven, somewhat surprisingly, to be the main entrance itself. A number of prisoners had created their own fake German uniforms and then walked out of the Oflag while posing as guards. One French officer had even dressed as a very convincing, respectable-looking German lady in order to escape while exercising in the park. Ironically, 'she' was given away by British prisoners when they spotted that the lady had dropped her watch as they were returning to the castle.

Other escape attempts from Colditz were just as bold, despite not always being successful. British Officer Anthony 'Peter' Allan had himself sewn inside one of several mattresses which were being moved from Colditz to another camp. Once his mattress was dumped in an empty house within the town, Allan cut himself free and went on the run, dressed in a fake Hitler Youth uniform. A fluent German speaker, he travelled the more than 300 miles to Vienna (hitching a motorcar ride from an SS official en route) but soon ran out of food and money. Unable to find help at the American Consulate, and suffering from malnutrition, he was recaptured by the authorities and returned to Colditz.

Several escape attempts relied on improvised ropes created by tying together bed sheets. On 12 May 1941, two Polish officers, Miki Surmanowicz and Mietek Chmiel, used such a rope to climb out of a window and down the 120 feet of the guardhouse wall. Unfortunately, their attempt failed when they were overheard and the German guards rushed out to apprehend them (allegedly shouting '*Hände hoch!*' to the prisoners clinging desperately to the bed sheets). Such an improvised rope also enabled British prisoner Dominic Bruce to escape on a different occasion, having been moved to an opportune location in the German *Kommandantur* while hidden inside a large tea chest. He fled the castle but was caught a week later while attempting to board a ship in Danzig.

Despite the castle's unorthodox location atop a rocky outcrop, several escape tunnels were dug. A manhole cover in the floor of the canteen allowed the prisoners to access the castle's sewer system and a drain was identified which, after being extended by digging, would exit near to the east wall of the castle. On the evening of 29 May 1941, a small group led by Pat Reid attempted to escape through the tunnel, having bribed one of the guards to turn a blind eye when they exited. Unfortunately, the guard had chosen to report the attempt and the participants were all caught in the act. At the same time, another much longer tunnel was being dug, this one by nine French officers, leading from the wine cellar beneath the chapel's clock tower. Running 44 metres horizontally to a depth of almost 9 metres below ground, the tunnel was only some 2 metres short of completion when it was discovered by the Germans in January 1942.

Tunnelling was also integral to an escape attempt by Flight Lieutenant Hedley Fowler, conducted on 9 September 1942.

It was decided to start a tunnel from the office of the Stabsfeldwebel, *this being the most unlikely place for the Germans to look. This office has a lock of the 'cruciform' type, for which we had made a* key, and is also padlocked on the outside, so that we had to be locked in by another officer every night. Six of us were engaged on the work – Lieutenant Wardle RN, Captain Lawton and myself, and three Dutchmen, Lieutenant Commander Van Doorninck, Lieutenant Donkers, and Lieutenant Bates.

Every night one of us would be locked into the office to work and be let out in the morning after camouflaging the hole. Finally when only about six inches remained we were all locked in with our equipment and one accomplice who was to replace the floor after we left, so that the hole could be used again by another party. We removed the last six inches of plaster and the way was then free into the clothing store, which was outside the castle proper but inside the wire and ring of sentries. It was quite common to see orderlies accompanied by German guards emerging from the store with bundles of clothing and we intended to dress as Polish orderlies, a German under-officer, and officer. We had made uniforms for the two latter, which had to be perfect, as we were to pass within one yard of a sentry in daylight. We had also made two boxes which looked like clothes chests in which we carried our civilian clothes. These boxes were made collapsible so that they could be pushed through the hole after us.

Once in the clothing store we plastered up the hole behind us and camouflaged it, and then had to wait for daylight and the guard to change at 7am, as the relieving sentry would not know whether anyone was in the store or not. At 7.15am we dressed the officer and NCO and made a few hurried repairs to their uniforms which had got damaged coming through the hole, and the rest of us put on dirty Polish uniforms and clogs. Lieutenant Commander Van Doorninck had made a set of skeleton keys and, taking the part of the NCO, was to open the doors and gates for us. At about 7.30am he picked the lock of the store, let us out, and then relocked the door in full view of a sentry who was standing outside. We passed two more sentries, who both saluted the officer, and on through the second gate. At the last gate Van Doorninck found that he had not a key *which fitted the lock, and we were just about to drop all pretence and climb over it, when a German guard arrived with a key and apologised for not being there before.*

Incredibly, the six men were then able to walk calmly out of Colditz, with the door being held open for them by a German soldier.

We were then away from the castle and made for a wood where we destroyed the uniforms and donned civilian clothes. The latter are always extremely difficult to obtain in prison. My outfit was a naval jacket, RAF trousers, and a workman's peaked cap made from an RAF cap and a beret. I also carried a small attaché case to give the impression that I was a workman on leave. We had forged papers the day before, leaving the dates blank to be filled in outside the camp. I carried an Ausweis or factory identity card with photograph and papers stating that I was a Belgian workman who was on 14 days' leave with permission to travel on the railways. Also as an extra precaution I carried a paper granting me permission to visit friends in the frontier zone. This I did not intend to show unless forced to, as we were doubtful whether it was necessary or not.

Once in the wood we split into three couples of one Dutchman and one Englishman and started off in different directions. Wardle and Donkers were heading for Danzig, Lawton and Bates for Switzerland via Ulm, and Van Doorninck and myself for Switzerland via Stuttgart. It was essential to get well away from the camp and to reach a station before the alarm was given. Roll call at 8.30am was going to be intentionally rowdy so that the Germans would postpone it and give us an extra hour's start. We walked hard for 31 kilometres and reached Penig railway station at 4pm. There we got a train to Plauen via Zwickau. In the train we spoke only when necessary and then in German, and our clothes were passable and excited no comment. We had stopped for a drink at two inns on the way and were not suspected, which gave us great confidence.

Fowler had originally estimated that they should reach the frontier in two days, but the poor wartime railway network meant that he was halfway short with his guess.

We arrived at Plauen at 9pm and spent five hours in the waiting room waiting for the Stuttgart train. We found that frequently trains on the timetable never ran at all and that others were invariably late, and for that reason it was very difficult to make connections. The Stuttgart train arrived and took us as far as Hof and there stopped. However, we were told that another train would be there in half an hour, but when it finally arrived it was six hours late and overcrowded with people. Instead of going direct to Nürnberg and through to Stuttgart, it made a detour through Bamback and Würzburg, and did not arrive at Stuttgart until 8.30pm. We expected to have to pass a police barrier on the station, but it had evidently been removed.

The two men now encountered one of the major problems faced by escaped prisoners of war, which was how to find a safe location to rest without raising the suspicions of the local community.

By then we were both extremely tired, and, as it was obvious that we should not reach the frontier according to our schedule, we decided to risk sleeping in a small hotel at Mühringen in the suburbs of Stuttgart, thus enabling us to be fresh for the 30 kilometre walk which we expected next day. We arrived at the hotel and told our previously prepared stories, which appeared to satisfy the hotel keeper, who showed us a very poor room with no blankets on the beds. Having satisfied ourselves that there was an easy escape by the window, we slept.

Next day we booked to Tuttlingen from a small station in order to avoid suspicion. Once again at Herrenberg the train stopped and went no further, so we spent all day in a wood waiting for the next train. At Tuttlingen we decided to walk to the frontier, as we believed that all the area 20 kilometres north of the frontier to be patrolled, and that travelling in it by train was too dangerous. We were stopped in Ehringen by an SS policeman who examined our papers and let us proceed without any difficulty. All the way from Tuttlingen to Hilzingen we used the by-roads, as we suspected that the main roads were patrolled.

They were already fully aware of the route across the frontier, as information on such escape routes had been shared among the prisoners in Colditz via coded letters received from home as well as other means.

We reached what we thought was the correct wood by nightfall and waited until 10pm before skirting round the wood and crossing the frontier. However, we had not gone quite far enough and started skirting the wrong wood, fording a stream on two occasions. We eventually reached the end of the wood and crossed a road, knowing we were wrong, as we had so far not crossed the railway line. About half a kilometre to the east we sighted the correct wood and, reaching the southern end of it, we waited and watched, having previously removed our boots. A patrol car came coasting down the road with its engine off and as we could hear (but not see) the sentries, we walked over a road immediately behind the car and 100 metres further on over the frontier. Heading due south we soon struck the fringe of trees and a Swiss Customs house, where we handed ourselves over at 1.30am on 13 September. We were taken to the town gaol at Ramsen and sent to Schaffhausen next day for questioning.

In recognition of his successful escape, Fowler was awarded the Military Cross on his return to Britain. Resuming his flying service, he would become a test pilot but was tragically killed in March 1944 when his Hawker Typhoon aircraft crashed.

The most ambitious escape attempt by Colditz prisoners, however, must be the plan to fly out of the camp by using a homemade glider. Constructed from hundreds of wooden ribs, adapted from bed slats and other pieces of stolen timber, the glider was assembled in the lower attic above the castle's chapel. The prisoners had already realised that the attic spaces were best suited for secret activities, since the Germans concentrated their search efforts on lower rooms where tunnels were more likely. The plan was for the glider to be launched from the castle's roof, using a 60-foot-long runway and pulley system to accelerate the aircraft to 30 mph in order to propel it across the River Mulde some 60 metres below. Weighing 240 lbs and with a 32 foot wingspan, the glider was no small effort. Flying Officer Patrick Welch was involved in the plan.

Any scheme for escape involved, very strictly, the cooperation of the people trying to do it and the escaping officer, whose job was to see if it was a sensible scheme; that it didn't interfere with anyone else's proposals; and justified or did not justify help from camp facilities. He wanted an assessment of the practicability of the glider, and as I was the only aircraft engineer in the place my job was to look at the drawings, do some stressing sums and consider it from an aerodynamic point of view and a launching point of view and say whether this thing would work. And that's what I did and it would work. It was a good, simple design, surprisingly conventional but they reckoned they'd got all the materials to do it, and as a simple little glider it would have flown. I'd flown similar ones in the past myself.

The launching method was cunning. It involved building the thing and assembling it for the first time in a long upstairs attic, v-shaped room which was going to be shortened by one bay. It was a very long room and so nobody would notice if it was shortened. This was done over one weekend when the Germans were unlikely to go in there because we had to go through three locked doors to get there, and a total false wall was constructed and plastered up to look like the original wall of this room. And that was the workshop, a triangular room that was about 10 foot in length of the building and I suppose about 30 feet across the bottom but it was triangular shaped. If the glider could be built it was then necessary to break down various bits and pieces of the castle and then assemble it on a very short sloping roof which was lead covered, which was out of sight of the guards from below. The thing would be assembled there, and meanwhile a launching platform consisting of a sort of telescopic wooden framework would be pushed out with a pulley at the end, rope attached to the front of the glider, coming back, and a heavy weight would fall down through various holes in the castle and catapult the glider off.

The scheme proceeded in great secrecy, with Welch working on the glider himself on a few occasions.

The building was done very thoroughly and well. Tools were available in Colditz, because once you got a file you can make practically any tool. Planes were difficult but a reasonable sort of plane was made up using an ice skate, as the blade is good steel. Saws were very simply made from gramophone springs with teeth filed in them as a form of bow-saw, highly effective and extremely good. The actual construction normally involved two people working in this room and about five people keeping watch, so that if any Germans came near the area, signals were made to keep quiet. And it proceeded steadily.

Yet the aircraft never flew, as liberation came sooner in April 1945.

By the end of the war it was fairly obvious an escape was rather fatuous and it was just worked more or less as an interesting thing to do at the very end. And then [on] the last day [it] was taken down and assembled for the first time, and only time, in its life. It had a

rather nice appearance... it was coloured with blue and white check
fabric, very small checks. The fabric would have been doped in real
life using the original 1900 construction material which was starch
dope like you use on stage scenery to shrink and tighten the fabric,
but that wasn't done. Anyway, it would have worked I think.

Welch was proved to be correct in his assertions, as a modern replica
of the glider was built and successfully flown in 2000.

Another audacious escape attempt from Colditz was witnessed
by Royal Marine Hugh Bruce. Bruce, who had been captured at
Calais in May 1940, was subsequently held at a number of camps
from which he attempted to escape. In August 1942 he was
transferred to Colditz where, talented in lock picking and bolstered
by his previous record of escaping, he became involved in a number
of attempts including what became known as the 'Franz Josef'
plot of September 1943. This ambitious plan involved replacing
two German guards on the perimeter of the castle defences with
disguised prisoners, thereby allowing a substantial party to get
away. It was anticipated that potentially the plan could result in the
largest and most daring escape attempt ever organised in Colditz.
The idea centred round the German Sergeant Major, *Stabsfeldwebel*
Gustav Rothenberger, who was known to the prisoners as 'Franz
Josef'. This was because of his large auburn-coloured Hindenburg
moustache which resembled the one forever associated with the
Austrian Emperor Franz Josef.

Mike Sinclair was the key man, and it was he who would impersonate
'Franz Josef' himself. His assistants were Lance Pope and John Hyde-
Thompson. All three were fluent German speakers. This ambitious
plan was based on the idea that Mike, dressed as the Feldwebel *'Franz*
Josef', with the others in German soldier's uniforms, would exit after
dark from a window on the north-west corner of the castle, which
looked out from the lavatory of the sick bay. It was tucked in close

behind the round tower there, and gave access onto the terrace path which was ordinarily used by the relieving guards. After exiting, the Franz Josef party would then march along the terrace path, and on the pretext of emergency orders from the Feldwebel, *relieve the No 5 sentry and then the catwalk sentry. Their places would be taken by our imposters, Lance Pope and John Hyde-Thompson. Franz Josef was nearly 60 years old and had service medals of the First World War including the Iron Cross First Class. He had a rotund figure and peculiar mannerisms, but the most important characteristic was his huge moustache. Teddy Barton, our theatre director, was asked to apply his make-up skills and he produced many fine moustaches, most of them out of hair which had to be dyed to the matching colour. However the one which was finally selected was made from teased out and dyed string fibres.*

Intense preparation was required. The plan was risky in the extreme, so nothing could be left to chance.

For weeks on end during those mid-summer months, there was intense stooging. Guard changes were studied, timings of movements of individuals were recorded, until at length the whole pattern of the guard routine could be understood and forecast. David Hunter and I joined Monty Bissel's team. Our involvement included help in identifying individuals, establishing details of the timetable for guard changes, and the composition of the guard company and their routine. We also had to take into account any changes to the routine or alteration to the siting of guard posts in the event of an air raid warning when the flood lights were doused. A great deal of other preparation had to be carried out. The German uniforms had to be made, as well as two wooden rifles and a sergeant-major's automatic pistol with holster. The only part of the pistol which can be seen when the holster is closed in the normal way is the black base of the magazine at the bottom of the hand grip. So that was the only part of the pistol which had to be manufactured. The pistol holster however was a little more complicated. To emulate the dull red leather, this was made from heavy cardboard and where the spare magazine case and the securing straps are attached, some false stitching was provided and the whole treated with dark brown boot polish to give it the right colour and appearance. In addition to these dummy arms, medals and badges, clothing and uniform had to be provided. Most of these items were tailored by Rex Harrison, all carefully and laboriously manufactured, and when completed all the outfits were so good that they could easily be taken for the real thing – particularly in the semi-darkness out on the terraces where they were to be used.

The date for the attempted escape was finally fixed as the night of 2 September 1943. It had to be a date when the real 'Franz Josef' was on duty as the guard commander, yet much of the rest of the plan had to rely on luck and the intelligence (or lack thereof) of the other German guards.

It was just before midnight that Mike, alias 'Franz Josef', appeared on his usual rounds, but on this occasion he was accompanied by two sentries armed with rifles. The sentry on the north of the castle was passed without incident. Then the Franz Josef party drew close to No 5 sentry on the beat up to the gate and Mike called to him. Then speaking in German, he ordered him to hand over his post. 'Two prisoners have escaped and you are required for interrogation. Hand over the keys and your post and return to the guard room!'

I was waiting at the window above this scene. I stood there with the remainder of the main escape party, dressed in my civilian outfit ready to go. I couldn't see much of what was going on, but it was a still night and I could hear most of the conversation. At first the sentry seemed to concede and John Hyde-Thompson moved to take over the post. *The sentry was handing over the keys when he suddenly thought to demand to see Franz Josef's* Ausweis, *which he was quite entitled to do, because the orders encouraged all sentries to do so. Mike handed it to him, and the sentry took it over to the light to inspect it. After handing it back, it seemed that at first he was satisfied and the guard party moved on towards the catwalk sentry. Mike gave him the same order, but just then the first sentry shouted at Mike to stop where he was, and he shouted a warning to the catwalk sentry, who went to the handrail and pressed the warning bell which was connected to the guard room. An argument started, and Mike became angry and remonstrated with both sentries, insisting that they should obey his orders. By this time however the sentries had him and the others covered with their rifles. Quite suddenly Unteroffizier Pilz, who was well known to us as 'Big Bum', came running from the guard room in answer to the buzzer, and appeared on the scene brandishing his pistol. He was accompanied by a German soldier who was also in a state of frenzied excitement.*

Mike was asked the password which he did not know. The Unteroffizier screamed at Mike in a high pitched voice: 'Hände Hoch! Hände Hoch!' *and Mike complied. Further argument ensued, whilst Mike was insisting that his hands were up, and as the real 'Franz Josef' appeared from round the corner with a posse of German guards, the Unteroffizier got carried away and in the struggle and confusion fired his pistol at a range of about three feet. Mike was hit in the chest and sank onto his knees. Such was the confusion that one of the German guards shouted* 'Mein Gott, sie haben unser Feldwebel geschossen!' *['My God, they shot our sergeant!']*

The three imposters were quickly arrested, with Sinclair being taken to hospital. The bullet had passed through his chest, but fortunately missed his heart by an inch. The other prisoners observing the commotion had to frantically leap into action. Bars on windows were replaced and camouflaged, while participators such as Hugh Bruce hurriedly hid their fake passes, clothing and money before assembling for the inevitable roll call. It was pandemonium and tempers ran high.

There were shouts of abuse, struggles and arrests. Subsequently several prisoners were charged with offences, and David Hunter was eventually court-martialled for shouting 'Murderers', for which he was convicted under the German military law code for 'Insulting the German Reich'. He received two months severe arrest at the German military jail at Graudenz.

What gave them away? Perhaps most damning was the fact that the escapers had created a fake *Ausweis* with the wrong name – the *Feldwebel*'s correct first name was Gustav, not Fritz. It also turned out that the format and colour of the Colditz identity passes had been changed only a few days previously.

German security gradually improved at Colditz as the guards became increasingly aware of the potential escape routes and methods employed by the prisoners. By the end of 1942, it therefore became much more difficult to successfully carry out an escape, and after the 'home run' of Billie Stephens and three comrades who fled the castle on 14 October that year, there was only a single successful escape from inside the Oflag before the end of the war. Escaping from the nearby hospital or while being transported between camps continued, however. The local gaol, located in Colditz town below the castle, was also seen as a good escape opportunity since it was considerably less secure than Oflag IV-C itself.

Francis Edwards, an officer with the 1st Battalion Royal Welch Fusiliers, had been captured in France very early on in the war, in May 1940. After various attempted escapes from several camps, he was transferred to Colditz in the autumn of 1943. No sooner had he arrived than he was caught up in the enthusiasm for thinking up a new escape plan. Edwards's particular skill was in lock-picking.

I'd made a set of keys, folding keys, which fitted the gaol. And I put them in a metal shaving-stick holder, with some money and a map, and the idea was that I would get through the German strip search with these things stuck up my bum. And then get down to the gaol at a time when the castle cells were all full when they'd put you in the town, so it was a question of timing. You had to wait until the castle cells were full and then get caught on some recognisable thing, not like mutiny or something, like trying to get out say. One hoped nothing else would happen to you, just given a stretch inside, a fortnight jail in solitary confinement.

So in order to get caught we had a plan with three of us. There was a fellow called Keats, a merchant seaman who was an absolutely brilliant shot with a catapult – a metal saucepan handle and solitaire marbles. What we got him to do was to knock out the glass out of the skylight over the canteen when the band was playing and he did a marvellous job. And then we got somebody to talk to the sentry. Then I was the tallest chap, I went out first, scaled up the roof and put my arm inside the skylight and lifted it, and noticed that there was practically no glass left in it at all. He'd simply taken every bit out. And so the other two came up and we got in and shut it and nobody knew that we'd done it. And then what we thought would happen was we'd try and tunnel through the intervening wall and set off the alarms and then we'd be caught and get our jail sentence. But in fact what happened was quite different.

We found there was a tunnel through the wall, with two steel traps at each end. It was an enormously thick wall. The steel trap this end was quite easy to open because you could get at it and the steel trap at the other end you had to prise, and there were no burglar alarms.

Edwards and his colleagues had therefore managed to get into the German quarters, adjacent to the main entrance to the castle, without any of the guards realising. Woefully unprepared for a proper escape at that moment, they could only attempt to deliberately raise the alarm in accordance with their original plan.

Early the following morning the other two, with a baulk of timber, managed to open the door enough to let me squeeze through, and I could drop down nothing more than six or eight feet into a passage. I had nothing on except a pair of khaki shorts, gym shoes and some cigarettes when I got through. If we'd only known we could have had a completely different plan. We could have tried to get out in a proper uniform, German kit, we could have had a go at getting out of the barracks! But we were completely caught out and the only logic was to get a prison sentence, to get run in.

So I walked round the place, it was very early in the morning and eventually I saw a German cleaner, an old woman, cleaning the passage floor. So I walked up to her and I said 'Is there any chance of getting a cup of coffee?' And she did a tremendous sort of double-take, let her jaw drop, and I pointed to the grinning face of one of my colleagues peering out of the corner of the trapdoor. And she turned round and there was quite a long pause while she registered all this, and then she let out the most ear-piercing shriek. Then the next thing that happened was a German soldier came along and rushed off yelling and then a German corporal arrived, absolutely bellowed. It was just like a pantomime. And eventually at 11am we paraded in front of the Kommandant of the place and awarded a fortnight's solitary in the town gaol. Which was rather a shame really, completely wasted but nobody knew that this was the one part of the castle that had no alarms in it at all. A great shame.

In the event, despite reaching the gaol as intended, the course of the war acted against them. It was 6 June 1944, and news of the D-Day landings soon reached the cells. With the opening of the new second front in western Europe and the subsequent mass alert among the German Army, any chance of getting clear of the town and making their way to freedom was extremely unlikely. So in Edwards' case, he chose to remain a prisoner at Colditz for the rest of the war. The American Army would liberate Oflag IV-C on 16 April 1945.

Rivalled only by Stalag Luft III's fame as the location for the 'Wooden Horse' and 'Great Escape' attempts, Colditz Castle remains one of the best-known prisoner of war camps from the Second World War. Officers held captive in the castle would write memoirs of their wartime experiences there, most notably Pat Reid, whose book *The Colditz Story* (1952) proved to be a bestseller and the basis for a subsequent film adaption in 1955. The superb BBC television series *Colditz* (1972–1974) also ensured that the castle would remain in popular memory, not to mention the board game *Escape from Colditz*, released by Parker Brothers in 1973. Stories of Oflag IV-C's prisoners and the ingenuity shown by their various escape attempts would come to epitomise for many the British prisoner of war experience.

8 | Work

Arbeit Mach Frei

The Geneva Conventions specified that officers and NCO prisoners of war were to be exempt from undertaking work for their captors, although NCOs could be involved in labour in a supervisory capacity. However, no such exemption applied to private soldiers, ordinary seamen and uncommissioned airmen who might all be asked to undertake work of some kind. Due to the greater capacity for industrialisation present in Germany, it was largely in that territory that most prisoners of war experienced labour in some form. For those men held captive in Italy, any work done was generally piecemeal, but this situation would change following Italy's capitulation in September 1943. Stanley Doughty and his fellow prisoners from PG52 were loaded into train wagons and transported to their new home as captives of the Third Reich, arriving at Stalag VII-A in Moosburg. They would now experience a new aspect of prisoner of war life from which they had so far managed to avoid – the requirement to work.

The shout of 'Raus – austeigen' ['Get up – everybody out'] told us that we had arrived in Germany. Thankfully, we staggered down into the fresh air, formed up into groups, and we marched away to a nearby camp, passing under a sort of triumphal wooden arch bearing the words 'Arbeit Mach Frei' *['Work Sets You Free']. A new and very different prisoner's life had begun.*

By 20 October 1943, Eric Laker and his fellow prisoners had similarly been transferred to Germany, this time to Lindau. An immediate improvement in their living conditions was balanced by the promise of having to undertake manual work digging in the local colliery. Sure enough, February 1944 saw Laker and 19 others moved to the nearby Kolumbus mine.

What a shock when we heard we were going there. Had to move after work, at 6pm, and we marched there. A bigger shock however when we arrived – 80 in a barrack room, wooden beds and no lockers. The first night I nearly died of cold but slept well afterwards.

Some prisoners made a concerted effort to escape work. As a lowly private newly arrived from Italy, the Germans were completely within their rights to put Stanley Doughty to work. Yet he had an ingenious method for avoiding such a scenario, by taking advantage of the chaotic situation caused by the Italian capitulation.

The Germans hadn't got the foggiest idea of who I was, since all the Italian records were lost, so that I could be anybody I wanted to be. In view of what I'd heard I decided to promote myself to corporal so that I wouldn't have to work for Jerry. Much to my surprise the British authorities in the camp didn't question this either. We were given a card to write home so I had to explain this to my parents in guarded language, and hope that they would write back accordingly so as not to give the game away. Luckily they did, but as dad explained afterwards they were very mystified as to how anybody can get promoted in a prison camp, but assumed that it was some sort of local and limited promotion.

With typical Teutonic efficiency we had been photographed and given a number and dog-tags at Moosburg. It was a relatively easy matter for those of us who were NCOs, of course, to dodge working by just not being around when names and numbers were called. Lists were pinned up on boards. Dog-tags were exchanged as necessary, and with it identity. So long as you had a dog-tag it didn't really matter whose, and the Germans never had the time to check tags against photographic records since the problem, for them, was on such a large scale and they were really only concerned with supplying the required numbers. You can imagine the fury of the logical and obedient Germans who knew this was happening, but couldn't stop it. All the British had to do was to act simple, which infuriated them even more for they just couldn't believe such disrespect for authority. Under their own regulations, to accuse us would require a properly constituted military court.

Prisoners of war undertaking work were often based at labour camps (*Arbeitskommando*) which were designated as sub-camps to the larger, permanent ones. From here they would be taken to mines, factories and other industrial centres in order to be put to work. One of the most popular destinations for prisoners obliged to undertake labour were farms, as recognised by Eric Monckton.

In the camp were many who went out to work on the farms in the district. This work may have been decried as helping the Nazi war effort, which no doubt it may have done to a certain extent, but the camp benefitted no end from such workers, bettering the health of the workers who got their principle meals on the farm where they worked and were able to escape from the dismalness of being penned up behind barbed wire. For people that were getting in any way morbid and affected by being constantly 'penned in', to go out to work on the farms was ideal. The camp workers were also able to smuggle into the camp quantities of eggs, poultry, onions, flour, fruit, milk, macaroni, bacon and all sorts of farm produce, at various times, though sometimes there was a rigorous search when entering the main gate on their return at night. The farm workers, of course, made a 'racket' out of their produce and if one was acquainted with any such worker, one bought the produce they sold when they came into camp with it. Cigarettes were chiefly the basis of purchase, though spare tea, coffee and sugar were very useful bargaining articles.

Originally held captive in Stalag VIII-B, Corporal Harvey volunteered to join a working party at a nearby site. Although an NCO and therefore not required to undertake work, he was keen to explore outside the confines of the camp and, perhaps surprisingly, saw the opportunity as a means to improve his living conditions.

We were mustered and proceeded to the working camp at a place called Blechammer, apparently some kind of a chemical plant being constructed. We arrived at the new camp in the late afternoon. It was like all the other camps with a high perimeter fence, armed sentry towers at frequent intervals, and comprised a number of brick built huts and a parade/cum sports space. We were allowed a day to organise ourselves and then we were included in various detachments and marched to the various locations where we were to work. The one I was allocated to was under the direction of a little man called Dickman, most unlike the usual blond haired blue eyed Teuton. It was civil engineering work associated with protective ducts to support some large pipe system and was on spare ground some distance away from the main construction. Without boring you to tears we could, with the aid of two metal sheathes, bore to about a depth of 15 feet, when the scoop was removed and concrete was poured in to create the pile. Our secret was to contrive to drop a shovel or two of earth in without being seen, to break the bond. Usually we could complete about two piles a day which brought

*us to mid-afternoon and time to march back to the camp. When
we arrived there the formality was a hand search, to make sure we
hadn't secreted anything resembling a weapon, also bartered food.
It was funny to see a man searched, with both arms above his head,
and what the searcher didn't know was he had an egg in each hand.
All clean fun to bring a smile to your face.*

As he had hoped would be the case, living conditions for the British
prisoners of war were actually better in the working camp than
back at their Stalag. Although the same could not be said for the
other nationalities of prisoner being put to work there.

*At least we were free from our particular friends, bed bugs, fleas
and body lice, for which I was very thankful. It was distressing to
see the Jews on the working site, little seven-to-ten-year-olds in the
horrible striped garments they had to wear, although the youngsters
seemed well fed and happy in their little worlds and I didn't see any
actual brutality directed against them. With the older ones they had
a much more worrying life. I saw one party coming on site one day
and they were supporting a comrade who was evidently very ill and
I, in my innocence, asked why they hadn't left him in camp. The
answer, of course, was that anyone left sick in camp was immediately
sent to one of the gas chamber death camps. Polish forced labour
people seemed to have a more relaxed regime and even though their
accommodation was near ours they weren't wired in or restricted.
This brings us to the last group in this area, the Russian POWs. They
had no Red Cross convention to protect them and they evidently
didn't get enough food to keep them alive. It was a common sight
to see them scavenging in the rubbish bins in the Polish area for
anything edible.*

One of the great disadvantages for prisoners of war set to work
in locations away from their permanent camps was the possibility

of experiencing Allied bombing, which often targeted industrial buildings and mine workings. Eric Laker was working at an open-cast mine near Lindau when the tell-tale warnings of an imminent bombing raid were communicated.

> *Excitement today! At 1.40pm the siren sounded and in the usual nonchalant manner we strolled to the shelter. A few minutes later planes were heard and we saw a wave of 12. AA fire began, and suddenly a loud rushing noise was heard. Bombs. The first stick landed slap on the Benzine factory which immediately started to burn well. We went into the shelter, the usual type of surface effort, and while there felt the place tremble several times. Coming out at 2.55pm we saw a colossal column of smoke from the factory, and one bomb had fallen on the railway line 100 yards from the mine. Coming back we saw a crater in the village street and several houses damaged. We also passed several wounded from the factory. Reports tonight tell us about 50 planes were here with fighter escort. We had actually seen the fighters weaving in and out among the big fellows. Our chaps did grand work at the factory, getting out dead and wounded civvies, and are still working there at 10pm tonight. Casualties among prisoners at No 22 Lager (300 yards from us towards the factory) were heavy – they work at the factory, and the complete death toll, which is very large, cannot be ascertained because they have not yet got out all the bodies, in fact they cannot approach because of burning and exploding tanks of fuel. The shelters apparently are useless, one collapsing on a company of German guards, and another on a large number of women, children and our fellows.*

The dangers inherent in prisoner of war work led to some captives taking rather extreme methods to avoid such labour. Stanley Doughty witnessed prisoners regularly embarking for the local work camps, which not only suffered regularly from Allied bombing raids but boasted a poor safety record among their workers at the best of times.

Some of our people would deliberately mutilate themselves, organise a minor accident to themselves, to get posted back to camp, in the belief that it prevented them getting involved in a fatal accident. The Polish mines had, and I believe still have, a very poor safety record, and the Germans saw prisoners as being expendable, and moreover had plenty of them.

Working patterns varied according to location and the nature of the labour, although as Tom Tateson made clear, there was seldom any opportunity for rest. The prisoner workforce enjoyed minimal rights and the Germans did not hesitate to get as much value from their resource as was possible.

We worked every day except for alternate Sundays, and we were outdoors throughout the bitterly cold winter of central Europe. Roll call was at 5.30am and we then went off in working parties to the moonscape of the vast open-cast coal workings, returning to camp about 4.30pm. A variation from work in the desolate surroundings of the opencast moonscape was provided when we were set to work filling the huge coal wagons with coal slack which had fallen and accumulated along the sides of the track in the surrounding woodlands. The smell of the pine forest was a pleasant reminder of better days, and the more enclosed atmosphere was a welcome change.

The long hours and intense nature of the work had a predictable consequence.

The question of escape did not arise in any real sense. Unlike officer prisoners, who had access to maps, compasses, expert forgers and more than ample time on their hands, we were a small working camp enjoying only one day off work every fortnight, and with no very clear idea of our whereabouts. I used to think that we were somewhere between Leipzig and Dresden, but in fact Bitterfeld is more or less 30 miles north of Leipzig and 80 miles northwest of Dresden. Occasionally one or two men would go 'over the hill' as it was called, but this was merely a sort of gesture of frustration, with no possibility of a successful escape. They would invariably be picked up almost immediately by the Volksturmer, *the German equivalent of our Home Guard, and would either spend seven days in the cooler or be transferred to another camp. Most of us preferred the devil we knew to the devil we didn't know, and did not want to be separated from our friends.*

One of the few advantages of being at a working camp was that additional clothing might be issued to the prisoners. The vast majority of men worked outside and had to brave the elements; during the winter months in eastern Europe this would mean below-zero temperatures, which were hardly conducive to effective labour. When he and his fellow prisoners arrived at Bitterfeld, Tom Tateson recalled how they were still wearing the same uniforms that they had been issued with when they left England in early June.

We had, of course, no overcoats and as winter came on our shirts and cellular underpants were dropping to bits, our trousers were worn thin, and our boots worn out. The weather began to turn colder and colder. There came a time when it was so cold that ice formed on my moustache and eyebrows. Before this stage was reached, however, the Germans supplied us with a bag of assorted old clothes. From these I acquired a pair of powder-blue flannel long-johns. The overcoats were mostly military ones and from every country in Europe. Mine appeared to date from the nineteenth century. It was single breasted and buttoned right up to the neck, with no lapels. The buttons were spherical and of brass. It was completely shapeless, and being somewhat small, came to just above my knees. I used a piece of thick string to tie round my waist, and the general effect was of a medieval working monk. We also received via the Red Cross a consignment of new British Army boots, a real godsend. Unfortunately, they were all large to extra-large sizes. To ensure the best distribution possible, we each took a pair several sizes bigger than normal. This was not as big a problem as it might appear, since I was able to pack mine with paper and so make them much warmer.

Tateson also benefitted from homemade clothing, as provided by fellow prisoners. Although sometimes a prisoner could gain more than he bargained for.

The Italians from a different part of the camp sometimes travelled to work in the same box cars as us, and they had for sale ear muffs made from rabbit fur; two shallow cups joined by a piece of elastic. In the coldest weather these kept the ears so warm that they sometimes became uncomfortably hot. Unfortunately ear muffs were not all I got from the Ities. One evening when I was resting on my bed I had a strange feeling of something crawling on my shoulder. After several absent minded scratching, I made a more determined grab and found I had a small creepy-crawly in my hand. The truth gradually dawned on me that it was a louse. I quietly disappeared to the ablutions where I removed my shirt, and on inspecting the seams closely was quite horrified to discover that I was lousy. I washed the shirt as thoroughly as I could, and returned to dry it near the stove, hoping that I had got rid of the beasts. The next day proved me wrong. I couldn't bring myself to confess to my room-mates that I was lousy, so I decided to report sick. This I did the following day, and my embarrassment was such when I had to tell the interpreter what my problem was that I blushed scarlet. This reaction to a fairly common problem among the Ities so amused the German corporal who was taking the initial complaints that he and the interpreter had a good laugh at my expense. It seemed that the Ities were known to be lousy and that was where my infestation had come from. Their reaction made it seem as though I was being over-fastidious, but the matter was in fact taken seriously, much to the dismay of the rest of the camp. Arrangements were made for us all to go through a de-lousing process on our next fortnightly Sunday off. This loss of a precious day of relaxation was very depressing, and it was perhaps as well that the fact that my action in reporting my condition was the cause, was known to only my closest friends.

After a few months, Corporal Harvey decided that he had had enough of working as a prisoner. Although he had initially volunteered to do so in order to enjoy slightly better living conditions in the working camp, he had begun to feel guilty about working for his German captors when not actually forced to do so. However, returning to his permanent camp meant a return to the poorer living conditions there.

So in a very downcast mood I prepared for bed that night to renew acquaintances with the bugs and fleas that were lying in wait for me and it was certainly a painful night. Having been clear of them at the working party camp I suppose I could be regarded as fresh meat to them. A round swelling was a bug bite and an irregular swelling was a flea target area. I have known times when things got so bad we would dismantle the wooden framework [of the beds], get a small fire going outside and pass each piece of wood through the flames to dislodge them but they would be back in a couple of nights. It was horrible to occupy one of the lower bunks because when the occupant above turned over you'd feel a plop on your cheek and that was a bed bug falling and when you crushed them there was a terrible smell.

As the war progressed and began to turn in the Allies' favour, a corresponding change in the lives of prisoners of war in Germany could be discerned. This was particularly noticeable in terms of the increased requirement for prisoner of war labour, as German industry suffered from Allied bombing and more garrison troops were sent to the front to counter the Allied advances, but also evident from the reduced rations being issued. These final months would prove distinctly bleak for British prisoners of war.

9 | Final Days

Now that it has come, it seems impossible – much too good to be true

For prisoners of war in Italy, the announcement of the Italian surrender on 8 September 1943 must have brought a sense of hope that their repatriation would be imminent. Following the Allied invasion of Sicily on 10 July that year, and notable air raids on Rome, popular support for the war had diminished rapidly among the Italians. Mussolini was imprisoned on 26 July and the new Italian government began secret negotiations with the Allies. At the time of the surrender announcement, Eric Laker remained captive in PG70 at Monturano, near the eastern coast.

About 8pm news flashed round the camp of Armistice with Italy and their continuing to fight with us. After this date we went out for walks unguarded but were ordered by British M.O. not to evacuate the camp generally. Parcels (food) and personal parcels issued unpunctured and unopened. German troops reported in vicinity of camp but only foraging parties proceeding north. Ordered to stay within safe distance of camp. Warned that we may be dive bombed and machine gunned by German planes on their way north out of it, but it is believed that the troops will be too busy getting themselves away to bother about us. Can it really mean that we are at last on our way home? Is all this caging up ended at last? My God I hope so although it seems that we are not out of the wood yet.

Two main Allied landings took place on the Italian mainland the following day, at Taranto and Salerno, and the troops began to work their way north. Yet the Germans had ample opportunity to send reinforcements to maintain control, and a new Fascist state was set up in the north of Italy under Mussolini, the *Duce* having now been rescued from captivity. The Allies soon controlled much of southern Italy and would eventually liberate Rome on 4 June 1944, yet the mountainous terrain in the far north prevented them from striking into Austria. As the majority of prisoner of war camps were located in the north, Laker's hopes of a quick repatriation soon faded.

16 September 1943. A daily roll call had been held at 9am ... we dismissed, turned round, and saw a German in the sentry box. When I saw that sinister looking steel helmet I felt as if I had received a violent blow in the stomach which fell to the region of my knees. I thought bitterly that it was much too much to hope for that we should have attained our freedom. It was all going to start over again in a different country. We were now prisoners of the Italian Republic Fascist Army.

Italy was thrown into chaos by the surrender. Wherever possible, considering their limited contact with prisoners inside Italian camps, MI9 had already sent word that prisoners were to stay put following the surrender. They desperately wanted to avoid the 79,000 British and American prisoners of war held in the country from running amok and complicating Allied efforts to gain control of the territory. The Armistice terms with Italy insisted that prisoners should not be handed over to the Germans but rather helped towards Switzerland for ultimate repatriation, but rarely did this happen.

The fate of most prisoners of war in Italy was simply to be handed over from one enemy nation to another. Italian guards were replaced by German ones and by mid-November 1943 roughly 24,000 prisoners had been transported by bulk into Germany in order to continue their captivity in a new location. By the end of the year this number had risen to 50,000. However, a lot of confusion existed, not helped by many prisoners of war choosing to escape when the opportunity permitted. For several months disorder reigned in Italy, with Italian soldiers returning home and hiding from the Fascist authorities, while local civilians often helped to hide both deserting troops and Allied escapers. By the beginning of 1944 there were still around 29,000 Allied prisoners of war remaining at large in Italy, many of whom would be rounded up over the coming months, although by October some 4,000 had managed to cross into Switzerland and 6,500 had reached Allied lines in the south of Italy.

Stanley Doughty and his fellow British prisoners held captive in PG52 were among those who couldn't resist experiencing a taste of freedom once Italy capitulated. Despite orders from their commanding officers that they were to remain in the camp and await the arrival of British forces, Doughty did not believe that the Germans would just ignore them or that the British could mount a rescue operation so far from their front line.

We had both seen and heard the German troops and tanks pouring southwards and were perhaps less willing to believe our leaders. It was a strange feeling to be free of the camp, partly wonderful and partly apprehensive. We now had responsibility for ourselves again and it was strange. We split up into groups of around 20 or so friends, with an undefined idea to stay up in the hills until our forces came along. In practice, it was well-nigh impossible to live up there. Winter was just around the corner; food could only be stolen from the cottagers who naturally enough were not too happy at seeing a couple of hundred hungry scarecrows around. The groups wandered around without any real plan just killing time and being a nuisance to the locals who must soon have reported us to the authorities for their own protection. Law and order from the Fascists had broken down. For our part, the first flush of freedom soon wore off in the light of realism, and we found the effort of hill climbing a strain. We saw the expected German guards arrive at the camp, and soon motorcycle sidecar patrols toured the immediate area, and it couldn't have been longer than a week or so before we were all rounded up again, the local population being very pleased to see the back of us. The Germans seemed to think it was all a huge joke.

Soon the prisoners' transfer to new camps in Germany began. Once again they would have to suffer the terrible conditions in over-crowded railway wagons as they chugged slowly northwards towards their new destination.

The truck was one of those all-metal ones so there was no opportunity to rip up the floorboards and drop on to the track as in all the best war films. In any case with our recent experience we were chastened, and quite willing to accept what fate had in store. I believe it was done at some of the more obscure local halts – we heard bursts of shooting and metal trucks were switched for wooden trucks later on. The whole train was now one of prisoners, including Italian prisoners, and puffed its way through the Brenner Pass to Moosburg, just outside Munich, taking about a week to do it. We were always being shunted on to sidings to let more important traffic pass, being allowed out only once a day to empty the big bucket in the corner of the truck used as a lavatory. If this overfilled before being emptied, the stench was overpowering and those nearest to it were drenched as the train jolted and banged forward. Nobody had washed for at least a week and only had the clothes they stood up in, and there was only standing room anyway. The physical presence of so many human bodies pressed up close to you becomes very revolting and objectionable in a very short time. With the doors continually locked and only small ventilators high on the sides of the truck the atmosphere made me sick which only made matters worse.

For all prisoners, whether newly arrived from Italy or already well-established within German camps, the war would continue. In due course, the conditions that prisoners of war experienced during captivity changed in subtle ways. Just as there was a direct correlation between the Allied defeats early on in the conflict and the confident attitude of their German captors, so prisoners noticed a marked deterioration in German morale following D-Day on 6 June 1944 and the establishment of a second Allied front in Europe. News of D-Day reached the prisoners in the working camp at Lindau, where Eric Laker was now installed, surprisingly quickly.

6 June 1944. The day we have been waiting for for months. Invasion. I first heard it from Freddie Brassington at work about 11am. Later in the day it was confirmed, and the camp buzzed with discussion and speculation. It must not fail! We had noticed when we arrived at the mine that the Germans were gathering in little groups and appeared to be discussing something most earnestly. We drank a toast in a variety of beverages – tea, cocoa, coffee – to the fellows who were doing the job, wishing them all the luck that's going; and a special toast to the fellows who would not come out of it.

Although life in captivity meant being shut off from the outside world to a great degree, it was still possible for prisoners of war to learn about the progress of the conflict. Letters from home could inform them to a certain extent, despite censorship limitations, while the arrival of new prisoners often proved to be the most accurate source for current information. Work parties allowed outside the camp might also have the opportunity to communicate with civilians who may impart useful gossip. However, the best source would largely be secret wireless sets, maintained within many camps, which allowed prisoners to listen in to BBC broadcasts. Eric Monckton recalled such a situation in Marlag-Milag Nord.

There were many good sources of news with the unofficial wireless sets that were made in the camp, the spare parts being traded from outside the camp by graft. One I saw was very minute, being made out of a Swedish chocolate tin. The sets had to be toned down to nearly a whisper so not to betray their presence to the Nazi guards that were always prowling around, and the prisoners had to post their own guards to give an alarm if there were any Nazis around. Therefore the news was subject to the memory and reliance of the persons that took the news and passed it on. The sets also had to be securely hidden as many were the raids on the different barracks by the Gestapo in their efforts to try and find the source of our news, for there were in the camp some informers, I am sorry to say. Fairly reliable home news was received and the progress of the war followed on maps of Russia and Italy, which were sketched by very able prisoners.

The distribution of news within the camp was often a serious business which involved a carefully planned network of contacts. Frank Stewart, held in Oflag VII-B at Eichstatt, described their efforts to receive accurate news. The big difficulty was in knowing how serious to treat the widespread rumours.

Since news of the outside world, and often the inside for that matter, is difficult to come by, rumours play quite an important part in prison life, if only by providing a new topic of conversation. Where and how they start is often impossible to discover, and that and the fact that by the time they have moved from one end of the camp to the other they have usually become utterly fantastic discourages one from putting much faith in them (the rate of circulation depends on the interest of the rumour but anything interesting normally does the half-mile in under half an hour). To be safe, the only sources you can rely on used to be orders issued direct from the German Kommandantur and messages from our own Brigade Office, but these are rare and usually identical anyway. Recently, however, a new department has been inaugurated which makes rumour-mongering a less amusing but more reliable activity. This is the Camp Information Bureau. Its office is in the canteen and anyone with any information he considers interesting takes it along. It is then censored by the two officers who work behind the bar and if they think it of general interest they stick it up on a notice board. (Incidentally the CIB is of great use in tracing books which you've lent out but which haven't been returned). The information is mainly extracts from letters received in the camp but they claim to be able to answer any question that's put to them.

Following D-Day, the war was being brought to the Germans, who were put into the position of having to defend their homeland for the first time. The news throughout 1944 continued to be largely positive for the Allies.

On 28th March the camp was very excited on hearing the news that the Allied armies had crossed the Rhine. The radio sets are in constant use getting the BBC news programmes, with watchers on duty to inform the receivers of news of the approach of any Nazi guard. Though the Nazi guard personnel seem to be relinquishing the strict guard over us and appear to be absolutely 'fed up' and downcast as they too have no doubt heard the news of our advances in their wonderful country. We are busy packing and making new knapsacks ready for the return to home and a civilized country. The guards are most persistent that they are not Nazis but Germans at this period and just await the capitulation of their war leaders.

With Germany on the defensive, resources were stretched and this was felt in particular by the prisoners of war. Manpower resources declined as the younger, more able German troops were moved to the front. Eric Monckton noted the difference that this made to the quality of guard present in Marlag-Milag Nord.

During the early part of January [1944] it was very evident that the manpower of the Nazis was declining, as the guards under 45 years of age were taken away from the garrison to active service on the battlefronts, being replaced by much older soldiers, some well over the 60 mark. The garrison soldiers were a very slovenly and poor example of soldier now, rather striking to us who had heard in past years what a wonderful war machine the Nazi one was.

Frank Stewart, in Oflag VII-B at Eichstatt, also observed the changes.

A number of the German guards have been taken away to the fighting fronts and have been replaced by members of the Volksturm. *These are the Home Guard and are dressed in brown overcoats. They are of any age over 50 and are being quickly trained. They often pass the camp in a column singing marching songs. I like these songs. They are very Germanic and martial and everyone has to sing. They must be good to march to. A lot of the training is being done in sight of the camp and it's rather a pathetic sight. They are under the command of a sergeant who keeps them at a run, giving the alternate commands 'Lie down, Get up, Lie down, Get up.' It must be heart-breaking.*

It was not just manpower which was under strain. Local food supplies were often redistributed elsewhere and there was a common shortage of fuel, limiting the amount of heat and light for the prisoners. As rations dwindled, the winter of 1944 proved to be a particularly harsh one, and prisoners desperately sought out spare wood to burn in order to keep themselves warm. To add to an already troubled situation, transportation difficulties resulted in fewer Red Cross food parcels arriving at the camps.

Red Cross parcels, always a rarity in our Stalag, became more so. The Germans explained that it was our own fault – our own people bombed the railways and so disrupted traffic. (This was never admitted in the previous three years that the bombing did any damage at all!).

Indeed, it was commonly believed that the German guards were seizing the contents of food parcels themselves in order to supplement their own meagre rations. Always ready to draw attention to what he perceived as the pitiable conduct of his captors, Eric Monckton recorded his reaction to an announcement in November 1944 that the standard prisoner food ration was to be reduced.

Bread, sugar and potatoes are to be reduced in amounts of issue and the meat ration issued to be changed from cattle meat to horseflesh. We are still on a reduced ration of Red Cross parcels, the weekly parcel for some time having been reduced to one parcel a fortnight. Sports have been given up as there is no stamina in the players. The standard of feeding is not sufficient for the maintenance of good health and stomach trouble is being met with in increasing numbers amongst us. The Nazi issue of food is one plate of soup at midday, consisting of 60% water, and with the ever present cabbage and potato in it. The dry stores (bread, jam, margarine, cheese, etc.) is all substitute foods and of no nourishing properties at all.

From 5th February [1945] the Nazi food ration is cut down by a further 25% and they are giving us practically nothing at all. Red Cross parcels of food arriving at the camp are nil, and only sufficient remaining for one month's supply. Private parcels arriving at the camp are practically nil. In the camp are now 3,300 prisoners of all nationalities and every hut is very overcrowded and some of the hut rooms they were originally accommodated for ten prisoners now have fourteen and sixteen in them, the atmosphere inside being sickening and foul.

Eric Laker was hit particularly hard, being expected to work for over ten hours each day in a mine without being given an adequate diet. As he put it, 'with no Red Cross food what the devil do these blighters expect us to live on – hope?' The situation only grew worse over time, with food shortages felt across the board in all prisoner of war camps, as Tom Tateson at Bitterfeld confirmed.

January and February [1945] were very bleak months. Rations were progressively reduced, and Red Cross parcels had dried up completely. There were always rumours about imminent deliveries which failed to materialize. We had heard that large stocks of parcels were held at Lubeck on the Baltic coast, but that the German transport system was now so disrupted that the chances of any reaching us were very slim. Being undernourished and exposed daily to the bitter cold, I developed a weeping sore on my face which spread round my mouth and cracked with any movement of my facial muscles. I began to despair of it ever clearing up. The meagreness of our rations at this period caused some men to look for supplements whilst out working. I even heard of some men boiling up grass which was pretty nonsensical. One of the Canadians however used his knowledge of the woodlands to snare a squirrel. This caused quite a stir in the camp and I went along to see. He pinned the carcass by its paws to a tree and expertly flayed it. The resulting puny corpse resembled a tiny new-born baby, and hungry as we were, I am sure I could not have eaten it.

As well as the lack of Red Cross parcels, mail in general was taking significantly longer to reach camps. The final month for prisoners' letters to be delivered was January 1945, after which they were effectively incommunicado with home until after their liberation. With the second front now active in western Europe, more Allied prisoners were arriving in bulk to fill the camps and living conditions deteriorated as a result. Allied aerial bombing also intensified, targeting nearby towns and the industrial centres where many prisoners were forced to work.

As the Allies advanced from the west into Germany and the Russians approached from the east, the expectation among prisoners of war was that their camps would be evacuated once the fighting neared their location. The worst situation was faced by those to the east, as the Germans were greatly fearful of the Russian advance and prisoners were concerned that they may be used as bargaining fodder. The Red Army pushed west into East Prussia and Poland, taking Warsaw on 17 January 1945, and was soon less than 100 miles from Berlin itself. Fearful of being overrun, the German prisoner of war camps began to evacuate to the west, and the first of many long marches began in January 1945. Originally intended to head towards Lamsdorf (Stalag 344) and Gorlitz (Stalag VIII-A), the many columns of escorted prisoners soon splintered in different directions, but with all of them heading away from the Russian advance. Even in the concentration camp complex at Auschwitz-Birkenau, inmates were marched out and packed into trucks.

In the case of Stalag XX-B, located at Marienburg, a forced march by between 9,000 and 10,000 British prisoners began on 23 January 1945. There was a wholesale evacuation of towns and villages east of Marienburg owing to the Russian advance, and the prisoners of war joined the constant stream of military personnel and civilian refugees moving westwards. Their journey would continue for the next 3 months, eventually ending at Gossa in Saxony and involving a total distance of 1,079 kilometres. The camp's 'Man of Confidence', James Fulton, kept a diary throughout their traumatic journey.

On 23rd January at 8pm, I was sent for by the Lager commandant of the main camp (Lieutenant Kohlmann) who ordered me to warn all British POWs to be ready to march at half-an-hours' notice as from 10.30pm. At 11pm we were paraded in the falling snow and at 2.15am on the 24th January, after having been issued with three days' rations by the Germans and carrying a good quantity of our own Red Cross food, blankets and other kit, we moved off from Lager Willenberg. Except for short halts, every two or three hours, we continued marching through the night and all the next day, along slippery roads. By 5pm, we had covered a distance of 33 kilometres. We were herded for the night into an open field at Spangau-Dirschau and ordered not to light fires. There was no issue of a hot meal, not even an issue of hot water. The men were tired, but the bitter cold (it was 18 degrees below zero) made sleep almost impossible. Some were so exhausted however, a fact which I attributed to their never having been out of the main camp for over four years, that they just lay down where they were and fell asleep. Realising that there was a danger of their freezing to death, I ordered some of the senior NCOs to move about and wake up those who they thought might be in danger of succumbing.

For the remainder of the march, barns were provided for sleeping at night for those lucky ones who could find room inside, although this offered little protection against the severe weather. Many still had to rest outside on bundles of straw, hastily assembled, which did little to guard against the elements. Much of the marching was undertaken during severe snow blizzards.

As a result, the following morning saw the first of the cases of frost-bite to feet and ears. As there were no doctors (British or German) with this column, attention was given to these casualties by our own medical orderlies with what meagre supplies they possessed. They worked hard against heavy odds. Carts were ultimately placed at the disposal of the sick but the Germans had their own ideas as to who was 'sick' – e.g. only those who had visible and obvious indications of their condition (large sores on the feet, etc.). All those suffering from dysentery and diarrhoea, a very common complaint, were curtly dealt with and left to drag themselves along as best they could with the help of a rifle-butt frequently administered.

It was not until the fourth day of marching that hot water was first issued, having been obtained as a result of bartering with personal possessions such as soap. Permission was also given to light fires, allowing those prisoners who still possessed some Red Cross food to be able to heat the contents of their tins; prior to this, the contents had to be consumed in their frozen form.

Sometimes I would manage to buy a horse, though when this was cooked and portioned out amongst hundreds of men, it did very little to satisfy their hunger. I spent over 500 marks for horsemeat and potatoes, being given a promise that the money would be reimbursed, but this promise was never carried out.

One of the worst aspects of the march proved to be the lack of sanitary arrangements, which led to inevitable consequences.

Time and again men were turned back when seeking even some cold water to wash their faces. As they could never take off their clothes owing to the extremely cold weather, it was inevitable that as the weeks went past, lice should make their appearance. This constant body irritation, combined with malnutrition, reduced the general health level to an alarming degree. Then again, latrines were non-existent. It was sometimes prohibited to leave the barns into which we were herded for the night. Sometimes permission was granted for us to dig shallow trenches just outside. Then again, we were forbidden to go out after a certain hour under pain of being shot. With dysentery and diarrhoea so rife, this sort of situation gave rise to the most bitter friction between the men and their guards and culminated in 'incidents' which just fell short of being converted into shooting tragedies.

Other columns of prisoners shared a similar experience to those from Stalag XX-B. In total, about 100,000 Allied prisoners of war marched into northern Germany, approaching the Baltic coast. Another 60,000 moved through central Germany and 80,000 were driven out of the southern part of the country. By the middle of March 1945, it was estimated that one-quarter of all Allied prisoners were on the move. Monday 15 January 1945 saw Corporal Harvey and his fellow prisoners from Stalag VIII-B begin their own evacuation.

We kept going in the ice, snow and bitter cold in the expectation we should arrive at another Stalag but then we were told we had changed direction to go deeper into Germany. I think if they had shot us and dumped us at this point and in these conditions it would have been a relief. Worse was to come because the change in direction to the west meant we had to cross the Sudety [sic] mountain range which was notorious for the extreme blizzard conditions in winter. In the barns at night we had to take our boots off to ease our feet and this meant the leather froze during the night, so the first hours march next day was in frozen boots. I had a towel which I wrapped around my head and face especially on this walk over the mountains where we faced snow driven by high winds. This must have been mid-February, nearly a month after setting out, the food in the Red Cross parcels had all been eaten and we were dependent on getting a bread allowance every three or four days, usually a loaf between six men. I clearly remember one morning, after a night in a barn, when we thought it was a bit warmer, but as we passed through a village a large thermometer attached to a building showed minus 15 degrees centigrade, below zero, not so warm.

We had long since jettisoned as much as we could to lighten our loads, a trip to a toilet was in the open fields, with the knowledge we then had to catch up with the column. Washing and shaving were a luxury we couldn't indulge in and I remember the discomfort of long facial hair from the neck and chin. Still we carried on, no longer marching or even walking just shuffling along, the column of the damned. A horse and cart followed behind for those who collapsed through exhaustion or illness. I presume those very ill would be taken to a hospital somewhere.

As well as the atrocious marching conditions, the columns of prisoners had to face the danger of attack by Allied aircraft, who were looking for German convoys to disrupt. It was a dangerous time. SS troops were sweeping the surrounding woods for deserters while camps in western Germany soon overflowed with new prisoners until eventually these too were abandoned as the Americans advanced. Tom Tateson was evacuated from a working camp near Bitterfeld.

My recollections of that march are few, but I do recall that much of it was on roads bordered by woodlands, from which we heard many rifle shots. Occasionally we saw members of the Hitler Youth movement, young boys in their early teens, carrying rifles. They were roaming the woods seeking victims such as forced workers from the east, escaped prisoners and deserters. A macabre sense of humour amongst us led to the comment, 'One more Russkie bites the dust,' whenever we heard a shot. It was certainly a deterrent to any who had thoughts of making a break for it. At one point the Germans started jettisoning quantities of records after simply tearing some of them up. Some of these were bagged by our men, who found individual prisoner's record cards bearing their 'mug shots' with a board across the chest recording their prisoner number.

Their dangers continued after arrival in a new camp. Activities on the ground were not always obvious to aircraft observing them from a great height.

The next day Allied fighters flew low over the camp and almost immediately afterwards returned and dived, strafing a convoy of horse-drawn carts leaving the camp. By this time the Germans were making little obvious attempt to guard the camp, and there was a rush of men to the place where a horse had been hit and killed. They returned bearing hunks of meat cut from the still warm body of the horse, and proceeded to boil these up. After the strafing incident, fearing that we might still be killed by our own side, someone produced a toilet roll and laid out the letters 'P.O.W.' in huge characters on an open space in the middle of the camp. Soon after, a plane flew over and flipped its wings in acknowledgement that the message had been read. At the time the thought struck me that a toilet roll was an unimagined luxury and wondered how it could have been produced.

For Frank Stewart and his comrades in Oflag VII-B, their evacuation began on 14 April 1945. Within only an hour or so of leaving their prisoner of war camp, the approaching battle made itself known. Six American fighter aircraft appeared and, diving low, began to drop bombs on a nearby road. Stewart believed that they had hit their target and moved on, yet it seems that the pilots were unaware of the nature of the column of prisoners marching below them.

It was then that the worst thing happened. Something that none of us had ever contemplated! The six planes appeared once more, diving low, but this time they were aiming straight at <u>us</u>. There was a roar and a spit, spit, spit and the next thing I remember was lying in the ditch with my face on the ground. The next quarter of an hour was hell. The fighters attacked with machine guns up and down the *column five times in all. The noise was deafening. It was unbelievable that they were aiming for us, but the whine above us and the rat, tat, tat of bullets on the tarmac road just beside us left us in no doubt. At last it was over and we scattered over the fields on either side of the road. Someone shouted, 'Get back to the camp', and we did, running as fast as we could, baggage and all. Back under cover I took off my kit and lit a cigarette. My hand was shaking like a leaf.*

Because of the danger presented by aircraft and the surrounding battle, Tateson's group of prisoners from Bitterfeld decided that they should just wait until American troops arrived to liberate them. However, they somehow came to realise that the camp in which they were sheltering was located in the direct line of the Russian advance, so chose instead to take their chances by trying to reach the Americans.

We duly set off again but we had not been walking long when rumours began to circulate that the German guards were intent on giving themselves up to the Americans, since their great fear was of falling into the hands of the Russians. This proved to be the case when we reached a bombed and almost completely destroyed bridge over the river Elbe. The Americans were on the other side (we learned later that this was, by agreement with the Russians, the limit of their advance). We climbed and scrambled over the twisted girders to freedom. Freedom was in this case a relative term, since we were now marshalled and confined by the American troops. The German officers and men were disarmed and made to march off with their hands on their heads. The volte-face was so complete it came almost as a shock.

For other prisoners of war, particularly those located in central or western parts of Germany, the impetus to evacuation the camps was not so acute and many, such as Eric Monckton in Marlag-Milag

Nord, were therefore in a position of having to simply wait for their liberators to arrive.

On 19th April about 9pm all prisoners were mustered on the ratings main parade ground by the main gate of the camp and an address was delivered by Captain Wilson RN as follows: 'Nazi Commandant Rogge has informed me that he is remaining with 100 guards to hand over the camp on the arrival of the British Army, who are at Zeven, some 9 miles away. The hour of liberation is at hand and they may arrive at any time now. So be joyful but not too exuberant. There must be no smoking in the open or any lights at night. There will be Royal Marine Light Infantry guards on duty inside the camp and nobody is allowed outside the barbed wire boundary unless on officially granted duty. I call on everybody to help me to carry out the orders and to make the naval guards' task easier.'

This strange intermediate state of captivity, guarded half-heartedly by demoralised Germans as well as men from their own side, was to last for just over a week. Then, on 27 April, the Allied armies drew nearer to Westertimke. From inside the camp, Monckton was able to observe the progress of their liberation.

The camp is now in a really serious position, with shells of all descriptions screaming over us and machine gun bullets raining about in the camp... A British tank coming along the Kirktimke road and proceeding to Lagers 3 and 4 put a shot into the farmhouse and two tanks taking to their heels and racing along the road... I noticed a lone British soldier creeping up from the south and east of the camp and when the tank put the shot into the farmhouse, he was only then some 50 yards or less from the back entrance of the farm, which faced the camp. As the Nazis came out of the farm back door he just mowed them down like ninepins. The farmhouse was wrecked by that beautifully placed shot from the British tank.

The battle went on until 10.30pm... British motorized units chased the Nazis along the road well to the west of the camp, in the direction of Bremen, at about 9.30pm. There still remained snipers at farms in the village of Westertimke some 500 yards to the north of the camp. There were lots of Mills bomb explosions followed by machine gun fire in the village and the lads were evidently clearing the farms of snipers and any persons that were inside. One could hear things bouncing down the roads, as if all the doors, gates, and window frames were bouncing their way merrily down the main road. It was just one mixture of bomb explosions. Machine gun fire, 'bazookas' and tommy-gun work. The village was cleared about midnight and then the Welsh Division of Tank Corps rattled up and placed their tanks at each corner of the camp with guns facing away ready for action if the dirty Nazi rats should take it into their heads to return for some more of the right medicine. Gun fire and tank fire goes on all night long to the west and south of us.

At last we are in the hands of the British and the joy of being released from our bondage is great. There were not many who slept that night and we all entertained the relays of tank personnel who could get off for a few minutes while their fellow crew kept watch on the tanks. When the soldiers arrived shortly afterwards, they shouted over the wire if we were alright and hungry and threw over chicken and even sheep from the adjoining farms.

The following day brought even further excitement for the prisoners, who were facing the reality of liberation for the very first time.

At 11am there was a muster of all hands on the main parade ground, with Captain Wilson RN in charge. The White and Red Ensigns were hoisted on the tall flagstaff on the square, amid lots of cheers by all. The USA war correspondents came into the camp and took photographs, etc. and gained lots of news of the prisoners' experiences. Later on we received our first bread for over two years, in my case, real white bread and not the filthy dark Nazi substitute with the husks, straws and bits of gravel in it. How welcome this bread was, and it came from the army field kitchens which were to the east of the camp. The camp now really went 'haywire', refusing to go on parade anymore and sawing down any trees for fuel, breaking open the barbed wire in many places so that we could go outside without any trouble.

For Eric Laker, imprisoned at Lindau at the southernmost point of Germany, liberation came much later than had been the case for others. The previous month or so had seen ever-increasing aerial activity over the camp, as Allied bombers brought the war further into German territory. But it was not until 7 May, the day of the German surrender itself, when liberation became a very real possibility.

The Russians and Americans had each broken through on the sides of us and were racing towards us. Just after we were warned to pack we heard heavy explosions very close in the hills, planes diving, and heavy machine gun fire. Lots of planes passed overhead. Smoke and dust seen rising in the hills. At 7.30pm we fell in, after much sweating and feverish activity (benefitting from experience, the first thing I did was to fill my water bottle), got to the gate, and were sent back. No move now – staying in camp. Got in the room at 8pm and heard a buzz going round camp like a swarm of bees. It's all over!!! It was. The day that I have been dreaming of has come at last. Now that it has come it seems impossible – much too good to be true. The jubilation of the Italy affair all over again and it was wonderful. Someone of course produced a Union Jack out of the hat. The loudspeakers tuned in to the BBC all the time now. Cease fire to be sounded at 3am tomorrow. Especially thick skilly to be served at midnight tonight. Issues of milk powder, pork fat and two eggs per man! Where it came from goodness knows. No more working under Germans at Hercules coal mine now.

The following day the prisoners rose early in the expectation of evacuating the camp and beginning their march towards the American lines. Eric Laker began to record the events in his diary as they happened, hour by hour, minute by minute, as the war suddenly arrived at the very gates of their camp. What had served as their secure home for so long was now in the middle of the battle zone.

7.30am. 88 mm guns just outside camp firing a few rounds. Machine gun fire heard. 8.45am. Heavy fire from 88s towards hills. Russian tanks at Johnsdorf (1 ½ miles). Warned to get into shelters as Germans are withdrawing and fighting a rearguard action over the camp. This is likely to be the sticky period. Small arms fire heard. Artillery firing all round camp. 10am. Firing ceased. Tanks apparently moving along Johnsdorf – Komotau road. Germans blowing up ammunition. Sections of German infantry withdrawing hastily along wire. We hear Bohemia and Prague surrendered at 9am today. 11.30am. A stack of unidentified planes circling and wheeling overhead. Single engine, fixed under carriage, and very large wings. Strafing heard in hills. 1.30pm. A mortar outside the camp fired one round towards the hills, and a minute later two mortar bombs landed in the camp. One landed ten yards from the side of our hut, and the other thirty yards away. Tubby Wordley was killed, and several fellows wounded including George Hawton who lost both legs and died later in the day. Bad luck this, after all the bombing and having nothing land in the camp, to get it on the last day and from our own people.

2.15pm. Rumbling heard towards Johnsdorf and I thought it was planes, but two Russian tanks went by. You may be able to imagine how they were greeted by us. We nearly went mad with excitement and streamed out of the gates as they went by. They went back later, and the Russian officer said we were lucky this camp was not wiped out. He saw the white flags which were flying from the huts, but

Jerry was fighting between us and the Russians so he ignored them, naturally and rightly so. Seeing us all walking about he thought it was a German camp, and was in two minds about wiping each hut out in turn. He said there is a proper procedure for prisoners of war, they either stand out in the open with their hands in the air, or are below ground out of sight. He says this area is now clear, the Yanks are 20 kilometres away, and the main Russian body may be going through here later. There may be a little more fighting, possibly some German shelling of the main body, or from pockets of resistance by suicide SS troops. I wonder if all fighting will cease at midnight when the armistice comes into force?

6pm. The main body started to pass through. Tanks, infantry, artillery, giant mortars, transport, masses of it. Brüx fell about two hours ago. Scenes of incredible joy by Czechs, all of whom are wearing arm bands. National flags are hanging from every other window. The troops as they pass through are throwing off bread, cigarettes and cigars, and being received with loud cheering. The boys are all walking about outside, just like the armistice in Italy again. All firing has ceased here now. Russian planes are circling very low, the Red Star plainly visible. What a wonderful day at last, although things looked a bit grim early this morning. 9pm. A long column of German prisoners marched into camp by Czech partisans. Officers about 12 in number, and 6 women among them. When the two tanks came by this afternoon, the Ukrainians who work at Kolumbus mine pointed out to the officer the SS boss who had made their lives a misery and also been a swine to our fellows. The officer raised his tommy gun and gave him a burst all to himself and he was still lying there this evening.

By the next day, 9 May, the battle had moved on. Yet the new balance of power meant that further reprisals against the German guards were inevitable.

All quiet around here today, apart from an occasional shot or burst, fired I think by enthusiastic partisans for the most part. I heard this afternoon about the Germans who were executed in the nearby cemetery. They were made to dig their own grave, were then lined up on the edge of it and shot. The man who was carrying out the executions had been three years in a concentration camp and had had nine brothers killed. The victims were high officials from Brüx and nearby who had been particularly unpleasant to the Czechs... BBC this morning told us to stay put, and officers will be here within ten days.

Many of the prisoners who had attempted to flee the Russian advance were slowed down by the poor weather conditions and the confusion shown by their German captors, resulting in quite a number falling into Russian hands. Just as Eric Laker's camp at Lindau was liberated by the Russians, so too was Stalag VIII-B at Lamsdorf, where Edgar Randolph had remained to look after the sick and wounded.

I was left in the 1,000-man compound with 34 patients; 3 or 4 sergeants, a couple of corporals and the rest plain privates – like myself. We were there for six or seven weeks waiting each dawn for the sound of battle and approaching Russians. The Russians, however, had stopped along the River Oder, apparently waiting for it to freeze solid enough to take their tanks and other vehicles. The Germans manned the searchlight and machine gun towers but had all the Stalag records packed on sledges at the main gate ready to run. They turned off the water supply on the day the others marched out. Luckily it was freezing weather and continued so whilst we were in the Stalag, so we got water by thawing out snow and icicles – which, as always in winter, festooned all the barrack walls. We kept warm by breaking up and burning wooden bunks and tables from the empty compounds. There were several compounds with

men still in them – about 200 of us altogether were left for the
Russkies. No rations were given to us, but the Germans allowed
half a dozen South African NCOs, who spoke German, to go out
and forage in the country around. We got a few tins of meat, piles
of Knäckebrot (a kind of biscuit rye bread and hard to swallow dry)
and some overlooked Red Cross parcels – not much, but, shared out,
was sufficient to avoid starvation.

It was a long, slow wait – we frequently heard small arms fire at
night in the cold, calm air – at 15 degrees F to 20 degrees F below
we were glad it <u>was</u> calm. On one occasion four Stormavik [sic]
fighters swept across the Stalag, held their fire over the barracks
and then (what a sweet sound) opened up on the German offices
and two guard towers, chopping the latter to pieces, including
their occupants. How we cheered them. We had tumbled out of the
barracks as we heard them coming – and one waggled his wings as
they flew off. Hardly the sentiments of a nurse, you may say, but by
then I was very, very anti-German.

In due course the small band of prisoners remaining in the camp
were required to evacuate. The second week of March 1945 saw
Randolph and his group of sick prisoners transported in cramped
railway wagons through Czechoslovakia and back into Germany,
looking for other camps with the space to take a handful of
prisoners. Most of the group ended up at Stalag XVII-A, located
at Kaisersteinbruch, which was a big mixed camp of Russians,
Hungarians, French and assorted partisans. It was here where they
would finally experience liberation, as Russian troops advanced
towards the camp, forcing the German rearguard into full retreat.

Just then a German 30-cwt truck, with four or five men in the back,
came roaring down the road from the ridge behind us. It rounded the
Stalag and went flat-out down the straight towards the bridge, firing
as it went, at the Russians, who had not yet reached the road. They

got through okay and roared on to the bridge. As the truck raced on to the hump-back the bridge was blown (by their comrades), flinging the truck 40 to 50 feet into the air, to drop apparently down into the river. Shortly afterwards two mounted Russians, each carrying a huge Red flag, galloped through the Stalag gates (opened wide for them by Russian POWs) and up the roads between the compounds, to show that at least we were free! Or were we?

This sense of unease was shared by many prisoners of war upon being liberated. For every prisoner who celebrated and looked forward to their imminent release, there was another who considered the situation more realistically and refused to accept the notion of freedom until it was irrefutable. Having finally escaped their camp after the friendly fire incident, Frank Stewart's party of prisoners ultimately reached Stalag VII-A at Moosburg on 23 April. They would have to wait for almost a week before the liberating American army arrived on the afternoon of 29 April.

A US tank came lolloping slowly up the Lagerstrasse, a swarming mass of howling bodies on top of it, followed by an impudent little car which I gathered was a Jeep. (We hadn't seen one before. Jeeps weren't invented till after we were captured). Immediately flags appeared from nowhere and were hoisted onto the bungalows, French flags, Russian flags, Stars and Stripes and Union Jacks. After four years and eleven months I was liberated. I went on with my book. The British must be maddening people. To others they must seem dull, unexcitable and abominably phlegmatic. Already the Russian compound is like the Lion House at meal time. Everyone is yelling and singing and dancing. For all I know, some may be weeping. The Americans are rushing round shouting and shaking hands with everyone. The British remain sitting in their bungalows looking self-conscious and miserable. When the Stars and Stripes was broken on the church steeple a crowd of Americans threw their hats in the air and began to cheer uproariously. An Englishman was standing beside them with his hands in his pockets staring silently at a large map of Germany stuck up on the latrine wall covered with little pins showing the last reported positions of the Allied forces. As the cheer went up he slowly raised one hand, took out a pin and carefully stuck it in the dot marked Moosburg. Then, with a shrug of the shoulders he turned and walked quietly away.

As for myself, I can't say I feel excited. I can't say I feel particularly exhilarated. I don't feel any different from what I felt yesterday, or the day before, or the day before that. I suppose the full significance hasn't penetrated yet and I don't suppose it will till I get out of here.

10 | Repatriation

A great placard was hanging up bearing the words 'Welcome Home', but I am afraid I could not see it very well. My eyes were too misty.

While the war was ongoing and before liberation was a realistic possibility, there had been only one pragmatic way for prisoners of war to be sent home. This would involve being classified as long-term sick or permanently wounded. The logic was that if a man was too sick or disabled to continue to contribute to his country's war effort, there was little point in him remaining a prisoner of war under the responsibility of his enemy. The Geneva Conventions included a provision for this, either as part of a repatriation exchange of prisoners or for the sick men to be transferred into the care of a neutral country like Switzerland.

The most common form of repatriation was through an exchange of eligible prisoners from either side. Eight such block exchanges were made in total by Britain throughout the war, consisting of four with Italy and four with Germany. Prisoners were selected by the camp medical officer or a senior representative before being asked to face a Mixed Medical Commission. This involved an examination of the prisoner, which would inform a decision on whether they should be considered eligible for repatriation. To even face the Commission in the first place was far from straightforward, while the subsequent diplomatic wrangling meant that the whole process was drawn out and frustrating for those waiting for a resolution. However, some 10,000 British and Commonwealth sick or wounded prisoners of war were ultimately repatriated in this way.

Some prisoners were so desperate to be sent home that they chose to feign sickness. James Fulton, who was the British 'Man of Confidence' in Stalag XX-B, recalled a prisoner who was determined to appear before the medical board.

> *I was always present during the visits of the Mixed Medical Commissions for the selecting of sick personnel for repatriation. On one occasion we had put up a lad who for over a year had feigned mental illness. One of his antics which annoyed the Germans (but gave immense amusement and fun to the prisoners of war) would be to come on roll call parade after the Germans had us all counted. They would be about to start a search of the barracks for the 'one missing' when he would appear pulling a small wooden horse with a long piece of string attached shouting 'Gee up' and 'Whoa'. He managed to survive the kicks on the pants and the cuffs on the ear delivered by the German sergeant major until he finally got fed up with him and left him entirely alone. During a conversation with the medical officers, they suggested they would put him in front of the Mixed Medical Commission which was due shortly to visit the camp and that I would plead for him. This was done, and it came as a complete surprise to him, to me and the rest of the camp when he was told by the president that he would go home with the next repatriation party. The same afternoon he was told he would be repatriated I overhead him saying to a comrade, 'My biggest worry now is to be able to prove I'm sane when I arrive in Netley Hospital.'*

Many other prisoners suffered from genuine medical complaints. Stanley Doughty endured health problems which appear to have been at least aggravated, but possibly even caused, by the poor diet he was experiencing in captivity.

My stomach was giving me more trouble now, and problems were also arising with my bowels, and eventually I remember vomiting blood on quite a substantial scale, I think, whilst down at the lavatory. I must have passed out, and don't remember much about the next few weeks, but I was in the revier (the Stalag hospital) with difficulty of sight, terribly weak, and with a headache to end all headaches. I was given two large blood transfusions by the old system whereby the donor had to lie on a bed beside you, at a higher level, and I suppose his heart pumped the blood to you. I have every reason to be grateful to the dozen or so donors from the UK and NZ who gave me blood which I'm sure they could not spare, and to the doctors who bothered under those circumstances, especially when I continually vomited again and again and the whole process had to be repeated.

The news from both the Russian and Normandy fronts was encouraging, and I eventually made good progress, especially when I heard that the Mixed Medical Commission was coming, and that I was to be included on their lists. This Commission was made up of German, Swiss and British doctors who, if they agreed, had authority to exchange prisoners who could play no further part in the war. The catch was that you had to be an in-patient if you were to be considered for repatriation, and as things were going it seemed as if I would be discharged back into camp by the time they had arrived. I had been feeling sore ever since the desert sand first caused trouble and circumcision seemed to be a relatively painless price to pay for the promise of repatriation, and so it turned out to be. With the connivance of the British medical officer I suggested circumcision to which he agreed and this minor operation was delayed and delayed until the Commission had arrived. It must have been 4/5 weeks I suppose, and if the Commission had been further delayed perhaps we would have thought of something else.

They did arrive and on the great day I and some 20 others passed. I had never felt so glad to be ill. In view of the scarcity of food most *of my sustenance came from liquid food contained in the Red Cross medical parcels, mostly Ovaltine, with the result that I can't face even one cup or the smell of it today. I was able to hold this down by now, and it kept me going. Men with open wounds had to be dressed with paper bandages and drugs were non-existent. Tooth extraction for instance was without any pain killers. Christmas came and went and we waited anxiously until at last the German doctor in charge gleefully told us that 'Tomorrow is the day.' Few slept that night.*

When the day of repatriation arrived, Doughty recalled his constant fear that the decision would be reversed at the final moment. It all seemed rather too good to be true.

Body searches and the last farewells from the medical staff and we were outside the gates, on a horse and cart, with a guard. I remember thinking, 'What do we need an armed guard for now' during our trip to the station, but I suppose that orders had to be followed. There we sat, in a draughty hut on the station, for what seemed hours before our train came in, and what a train. It seemed to be composed of coaches, not trucks, from all the railways of Europe, in various stages of disrepair. Some prisoners were already on board from other camps and I suppose we made the number up to about 200. Quite a number of stretcher cases, travelling on the floor, and the rest of us, the 'walking wounded' as we were termed, on seats which had undoubtedly seen better days. The atmosphere was electric, only dampened somewhat by our companions saying that they had already been two days on the train. We were soon to discover the truth of this when eventually the train jolted and jarred its way to the Swiss frontier. We collected one more lot of prisoners and were about ten days on the train altogether...

This travelling menagerie pulled into German Konstance station one morning early amidst great excitement. Hopes were high and eyes were bright. The platforms were decked with bunting and a military band was tuning up. Both seemed incongruous in the Germany we had seen during our trip; bombed and wrecked transport and railway systems; smashed towns, and shortages of practically everything. To this day, I think that it is incredible that the Wehrmacht could even think of this trip, with all its supply problems, under these circumstances. Within a half hour, without any fuss or noise, an electric train pulled in, and such a train that could only be a dream. Clean, externally and internally, like a vision from another world, and from it descended or were carried the German prisoners which were to be our passport to freedom. They looked well enough, apart from their injuries. The military band struck up; there was a speech of welcome; they were all given something in a paper bag, and were then carried away in a fleet of horse-drawn carts. Now, we thought, it would be our turn. We would all be moved into this splendid unreal palace, and move quickly through Switzerland.

To their dismay this did not happen. Minutes dragged by.

The band packed up and moved off and to our horror the train silently moved off back to Switzerland without us. The despondency and fear could be felt as solid as a brick, but luckily we were not left long in doubt. Just as silently as the other, a new train came into the same platform as the last, again like a vision from a world long forgotten, and into this, after final counting and identification, we were helped. Our guards left us, and without a sound the train moved off across a bridge, and pulled up again very shortly with the station sign reading 'Constance (Suisse)'. We had made it. The train was immediately invaded by English-speaking nurses in Red Cross uniforms, who helped us out on to the platform which was devoid of the public. It had been rigged up with showers and toilet facilities, and we were given soap and a towel. Never had a wash been so good. About an hour later we were back in the train in which we now found English-language papers and magazines on little tables between the seats; clean white head rests on the back of the seats, and a cloth bag on every seat. These were a gift from Switzerland, the bags containing amongst other things a small block of chocolate which they could ill afford, and I thought rather incongruously, a small lace-edged handkerchief. Red Cross nurses boarded the train and we were off. The contrast between our past life and this heaven where we were actually treated as human beings instead of numbers, left me with an undying admiration of the Swiss nation. They could have just passed us through, but instead they treated us like honoured guests.

Such wartime repatriations were relatively few, however, and most prisoners of war would have to wait until liberation to begin their journeys home. As we have seen, Frank Stewart had felt distinctly underwhelmed when his camp at Moosburg was liberated by the Americans. Like many prisoners of war, he felt a numb unreality about the whole situation and still couldn't quite accept that he was soon to gain his freedom. Considering the subsequent delays in his journey home, this sense of disappointment was perhaps somewhat justified.

It is a week since we were released and it has been a week of hell. Eight days ago we were POWs in the hands of the Germans. Then for four days we were ex-POWs in the hands of the Broons [Stewart's term for officious British officers]. Now our official title is 'Allied POWs under US military control' and the difference is negligible. We were released on the Sunday. All Monday we waited for the US evacuation staff to arrive, but the only people who came were a War Crimes Investigation Team who set up their quarters in the Kommandantur. *On Tuesday morning an American colonel drove in and announced that he was in charge of evacuating the camp and hoped to clear it inside a week. He was closely followed by a representative from Supreme Allied HQ who said that as we were the largest collection of prisoners yet liberated <u>he</u> was going to deal with our evacuation personally and* *hoped to clear the camp in six days. They both departed. In the afternoon General Patton himself walked in with red all over him and a pearl-handled revolver dangling from his belt. 'Hell', he said, 'this is a son-of-a-bitching awful place,' and when asked when we'd get away replied, 'Just as goddam soon as is humanly possible'. He then congratulated us on our discipline and returned to the battle. In the evening four American Red Cross nurses arrived; it was announced that a doughnut machine had been set up which could produce 1,000 doughnuts an hour, only there was no flour so we couldn't expect doughnuts for at least two days; then a convoy of lorries roared in and took away the sick – about 1,500 of them – who were flown home within a few hours. Things were looking up.*

Meantime, the Broons had taken over. Parades took place at 8am as promised, and lasted twice as long as the German ones. No lorries came in to collect refuse and the latrines clogged up and, for the first time throughout our captivity there was no issue of bread, though it must have been hard on the US Army Quartermaster suddenly to find an extra 70,000 on his ration roll. Worst of all, a new system of guards was inaugurated. The American prisoners refused to have anything to do with this, so the lot fell to us. There were now two rows of guards, one on the inside of the wire to prevent the wooden posts holding up the wire from being removed for fuel, and one on the outside of the wire supposedly to stop people from getting out of the camp, but as the people inside were armed with wire cutters, saws and axes, and the guards outside had no weapons at all and wouldn't have used them if they had, it was a bit of a farce.

However, Frank Stewart did experience a welcome but rather unexpected surprise.

When we were captured originally we all had a few oddments in our pockets which were removed from us. In my case, though I must say I'd completely forgotten about them, I had a key ring (without any

keys attached to it) and a small cigarette lighter in the shape of a
heart in red enamel which I'd picked up somewhere in France. When
we were liberated, all our belongings were found neatly placed in
pigeon-holes in the Kommandantur *with our names and numbers*
attached. So I have received back my key ring and my heart-shaped
cigarette lighter. The lighter doesn't work, of course, but then it
didn't when I was in France either. The Germans are a strange race.
Though they can commit the most ghastly crimes against humanity
without turning a hair, they are meticulously honest when it comes
to small things like this. These two trinkets have followed me round
for nearly five years through seven camps from Bavaria to Poland
and back. Amazing.

The end of the war saw the liberation of almost 170,000 British and
Commonwealth prisoners. The three main ex-prisoner-of-war transit
camps were located in Antwerp, Brussels and Reims. Arriving at one
of these locations, the liberated prisoner would face a debriefing by
representatives from MI9, which most men accepted but often sullenly,
perhaps reflecting their reluctance to return to service discipline.
Some preferred to answer the interrogator's questions with just 'yes'
or 'no' in the hope that they might then be transferred home as soon
as possible, while others used the opportunity to record in great detail
their various grievances about captivity. In their published history
of MI9, Michael Foot and Jimmy Langley noted with amusement
how the interrogators suffered from a spate of stolen pencils; long-
term prisoners of war displayed an automatic inclination to 'acquire'
anything when the opportunity arose.

The administration at these transit camps was rather haphazard
and any chance of recording a complete roll of repatriated prisoners
therefore proved to be impossible. Liberated men might arrive at
any time of the day or night, often requiring medical treatment,
food or washing, and were sometimes moved on to the next leg of
their journey home before any proper record could be taken. Of the

166,000 British and Commonwealth prisoners alive in Germany at the end of the war, only about 54,000 filled in the MI9 forms. The process was formally stopped in August 1945.

The fate of Allied prisoners of war who were not directly liberated by the British or Americans was far from straightforward. In the confusion of the final weeks of the Second World War, many prisoners escaped from their German captors and fled eastwards towards the Soviet advance. There was much disorder during the final days of fighting, no less the incident in which the Red Army overran Stalag III-B and killed some 50 American prisoners of war and wounding hundreds more, believing them to be Hungarians. Eastern Europe was full of many different combatant groups – German, Jewish, Polish, Russian and Ukrainian – who would readily fight any of the other four. An English-speaking escaped prisoner would therefore have simply been walking into trouble, yet Major Norman Crockatt, the Head of MI9, calculated that in fact one in every seven successful escapers from Germany in those final days of the war ended up in Russian hands.

Edgar Randolph had not joined the main evacuation of prisoners from Lamsdorf due to his remaining to look after sick comrades. As a result, he had joined the evacuation rather too late to reach American or British lines and had been 'liberated' by the Russians. Effectively this meant just a new form of captivity, less strict perhaps than that experienced under the Germans but still far from the true freedom which a prisoner might hope for.

At noon a Russian officer came and told us to move out and east. When asked what transport was available he just told us, in German, to use our feet – Budapest was 250 kilometres east – get going! 'Food?' we queried. The answer was sharp and clear: 'Do as we do, get it where you can.' So, out on the road, over the ridge eastward and on to Hungary – past Neusiedler See, a large lake on our left. On the flat land ahead we caught up with a column of refugees, mostly very old men and women. As we closed with their rear, two Messerschmidt 109s ripped across on their way home and, as usual with MEs, loosed off a burst each as they passed. Luckily, the planes crossed at right angles – the place would have been a shambles had they flown along the road. There was one casualty. A very old woman received a leg wound. The civilians angrily refused our offer of help, so we pushed on ahead. Twelve hours and twenty-two kilometres from the start, we were allowed (at midnight) to camp in a burning and deserted village. Evidence everywhere of looting. A real mess. We moved on next day about five kilometres to Haltbahn, where we were deloused (how lovely to shower in hot water) and grouped for a day or so, then sent on our way towards Budapest. Myself and ten patients were left – a couple of sergeants and the rest privates.

On 13 April, Randolph's small band of prisoners arrived in Soviet-occupied Budapest, four years to the day since his arrival in mainland Europe as a prisoner of war.

We came across a big posh hairdressing salon, so I decided to have my hair cut. Not having had the pleasure of this for well over a year I was really shaggy! My offside said, 'What about money, we haven't a bean?' I replied that we were not 'Kriegies' anymore and we were 'on top', so who wanted money? We marched in. There were six chairs – five occupied – and women getting hair-do's at the back. A barber came up, bowing and smiling (could it be my Aussie hat, again impressing people?). I intimated, in the Stalag German I spoke, what I required, sat down and he started. What a haircut! He did everything but throw out the fleece. When he had finished I stood up and picked up my hat. He spoke in Hungarian. I shrugged. He spoke again and I said in German that I had no money. He screeched and out came the manager and three or four of his confreres. Just then my friend said, 'Try them with soap. You have a piece.' So I fished out a treasured cake of Yardley's Lavender, still in its paper (it was from an early Red Cross parcel and was saved for some future momentous occasion). I said in German, 'English soap?' The manager gingerly took it and smelt it. An ecstatic smile spread over his face. He held it round to all and sundry to savour this delightful scent, then said 'Ja, ja,' handed it to my barber, spoke in Hungarian and the barber rang up the till, put the soap in and gave me ten pengos change! A graceful withdrawal by the troops and bang went the ten pengos on ten Hungarian cigarettes – black ones that made our heads swim and our eyes water.

In due course his small band would receive orders to proceed to Odessa by train for interrogation, and then ultimately repatriation. A useful summary of the prisoner of war situation in Europe during this time was given by Sir James Grigg, the Secretary of State for War, when answering questions in Parliament on 29 May 1945.

The repatriation of prisoners was undertaken as soon as they were reached by the British and American Armies, and very large numbers were flown back to this country within a very few days of their release. The Soviet authorities were meanwhile evacuating to Odessa those British prisoners which they had overrun in western Poland and eastern Germany. In the last days of German resistance considerable numbers of British prisoners were reached by the Russians in Saxony, Bohemia and Austria. When the Soviet forces had linked up with the American and British forces it was clearly desirable to transfer the prisoners directly rather than to take them round by Odessa. The local Russian commanders, however, had no instructions to do this, and as they were anxious in the interests of the prisoners themselves that the transfers should be orderly they prevented the men making their own way westward. An agreement for the transfer of prisoners was reached on 22nd May and has been going on since. As a result it is unlikely that there is still any appreciable number of British prisoners in the Soviet zone except in Austria.

The overall position now is that 156,000 British Commonwealth prisoners have been repatriated, over 140,000 of them by air. About 10,000 are awaiting repatriation either in General Eisenhower's or Field Marshal Alexander's zone and about 400 in Odessa. It is known that about 8,500 are in the part of Austria controlled by the Red Army, and it is hoped that arrangements will soon be made for their transfer to the British or American forces. There must be a number of stragglers on the continent whose collection and repatriation will take some time, and it is therefore impossible at the moment to estimate how many prisoners cannot be accounted for. The number is not likely to be large.

Most prisoners liberated by the British or Americans were flown back home to Britain. Tom Tateson was to catch a flight to Brussels first, before boarding another aircraft for home.

Having arrived at Halle we were assembled on the air field and told that planes would be arriving to take us to Brussels. There were many hundreds, even thousands perhaps, of men waiting. Time went by and pessimism took over. The planes would not come and we should be taken back, or to some other dumping place. Then suddenly a cry went up as three planes were spotted coming towards us. They circled round, landed, were immediately loaded up with men and took off again without their engines being switched off. By this time more planes were arriving and soon there was a constant stream of planes landing and taking off again in incredibly quick succession, so that the sky seemed to be full of planes. They were Dakotas, the small planes which were the workhorses of the Allies during the Second World War. I took my seat by one of the small windows, intent on seeing the destruction wrought by our bombers as we passed over the Ruhr. As it turned out, the realization that this really was freedom at last induced in me a sense of reduced tension, of anti-climax, and I simply fell asleep, only to awaken when we came in to land at Brussels. Here we received the warm welcome we had so far missed. We were issued with new clothes and were allowed to help ourselves from a shop run, I think, by the Red Cross, which displayed soap, toothpaste, toothbrushes, writing paper and many other things commonly regarded as basic necessities, but to us, great luxuries. It was understandable, if disappointing, to see some men helping themselves to handfuls of toothbrushes for instance. It was really like letting children loose in an Aladdin's cave. Our stay in Brussels was very short and soon I was looking down from our homeward bound plane on the incredibly lush green fields and neat picturesque villages of southern England. The contrast with the barren wasteland of the 'Grube Golpa A.G.' open-cast workings of Bitterfeld was so intense that I felt that I would never again, willingly, leave England.

Eric Monckton had a similar experience, his flight home leaving on 12 May.

Travelling in the Lancaster bomber at nearly 200 miles per hour, it was very noisy indeed, but we enjoyed every minute of it and the trip could not be fast enough for us. We were at 1,500 feet in altitude for most of the journey and it was a fine day so that we were able to see all the interesting points of land and cities all the way. We arrived at Dunsfold about 5.30pm and had a wonderful reception, the Red Cross representatives meeting us and escorting us to the large hall that was laid out for the meals of some several hundreds of returning. I shall not forget the man that welcomed me, he was a Red Cross representative and he insisted that he should carry my knapsack of belongings and took me by the arm showing me the way to the room where we were 'deloused' with the DDT spray. This was the third time that I had been so treated and coming from such a filthy country, it was absolutely necessary and the performance was not irritating at all. Dinner was then arranged in the RAF officers mess attached to the aerodrome and that was a good meal indeed, the first one on my native soil for some three years.

About six of us left at 7.30pm in an RAF small lorry for the reception camp at Chalfont St Giles outside London. We made several calls at the country 'locals', after we had got outside the military area and so that the driver would not get into trouble. We reached the reception camp at 11 pm and were met by the Manager of the Reception Committee who was very kind and helpful in every way. The first thing I did was to have a bath, the first one for a couple of years, and it was lovely to lie and soak in comfort, afterwards bundling my underclothes which were covered with the DDT powder into a bundle and putting them in the old clothes box in the bathroom. Then with fresh clean clothes on we went down to a nice supper and then to bed in real comfort.

Others found their flight home far from straightforward. Promised a plane ride to England, Frank Stewart and his fellow ex-prisoners of war from Oflag VII-B assembled at an improvised airfield. It was 7 May 1945.

At 10.30am one plane arrived amid a great cheer, and at 11.30am three more. By this time I'd worked out that with 28 to a plane we should be going in the 101st plane, and as we were told that 200 more were expected the prospects were looking good. At 12.30pm things started to happen. Someone sighted a plane in the distance, then another, and another, and in they came from every direction, great big moths flying low. Round the airfield they circled slowly and then down along the runway, swinging round into line at the end. Immediately 28 smiling prisoners clambered into the first one and off they went. In the first hour 40 planes came in and during the next hour another 40. As each one grounded someone called out the number. Already we had got to No 80 and were nearing the magic No 101. It was a wonderful sight and very, very exciting. We lay in the boiling sun, just looking.

The last plane had landed at 2.30pm. By 4pm the airfield was clear. For an hour and a half no more had arrived and we began to get worried. We lay around 'till 5pm, and then we got a shock. We were suddenly told that we hadn't only 21 planes to go after all. The order of leaving had been changed and 1,750 Americans were to embark ahead of us. We were back to where we had originally started and still needed 101 more planes to arrive. We waited 'till 6pm when we were told that no more were expected today. Sorrowfully we picked up our baggage and walked into the town to look for a billet. Someone said it had just come over the BBC that the war had ended. I'm afraid we laughed.

Eric Monkton, however, had been more fortunate. Having reached England, he was at the reception camp at Chalfont St Giles and only a few bureaucratic procedures remained before he could depart on the last leg of his journey home.

May 13th was a busy day, getting x-rayed to see that I was in perfect condition which, thank heaven, I was, except that I had lost three stones in weight and was as thin as a rake. I then attended the hut where I obtained my ration cards, identity card, etc. and went to a store to get fitted out. As I had clothes at home I did not waste time in getting suited for a suit of clothes, but got a mackintosh and an attaché case, then went and drew enough money to see me to my home in Lydney in Gloucestershire. I phoned up my brother in London, who came out in his car and took me off at 2pm to his home in London, where I whiled away the hours until the night-mail train from Paddington home. Arriving at Lydney station at 1.45am I got out of the train and proceeded to the barrier of the platform, passing my wife who did not at once recognize me, as I was still wearing battle dress and was so thin. We did however in a short time recognize each other and in no time were in the motorcar for our home.

When Frank Stewart finally reached England, the differences to be seen when compared to pre-war life were striking. The nation had changed dramatically over the last five years as the war had deeply affected every level of society, and for somebody like Frank who had not experienced civilian life for such a long time, the differences were quite vivid.

We were let loose at last on Thursday 10th May armed with rail passes, ration books and clothing coupons, and even a little cash in our pockets. Our first stop was London and, for some reason or another, I and a few friends headed for Hyde Park Corner and sauntered through St James's Park. I remember how we were all surprised, and indeed shocked, by the blatancy of the couples on the benches and on the ground, as we thought back to pre-war days when holding hands in public was considered rather daring. Also, we noticed how many women now wore trousers, a habit previously confined to the elegant set with their bell bottoms (the trousers, not the girls). We moved onto Piccadilly Circus and stood there in silence, recalling the scene. The lights weren't on again yet (it was too early in the day anyhow) but there was a great bustle of people. We thought they looked tired and drawn as they had every reason to be after what they'd endured from the flying bombs and rockets. I wondered what the Londoner at that time would think if he knew of our less vindictive feelings towards the Germans.

As we have seen, for those Allied prisoners who had fallen into Soviet hands at the end of the war the situation was far from clear cut. Still held by the Russians, Edgar Randolph had finally reached Odessa where he was promised eventual repatriation.

We were interrogated by the Russians (with a British Colonel as Prisoners' Friend) during which we admitted absolutely nothing untoward whilst guests of the Germans. We had been quietly warned that anything serious would mean being kept as witnesses for future trials and, as our treatment by our present hosts had not been conducive to any longing to stay with them more than was absolutely necessary, 'mum' was the word passed around. We got clean British clothing and waited for a ship. On May 1 there were big parades all morning in Odessa's Red Square – big deal! We were marched at the height of the 'hoo-ha' to the docks. We out-marched the Russkies through the Red Square, attracting quite a lot of attention. At the dock we boarded the SS Bergensfjord at 9am. The ship was Norwegian with her own crew and officers and she had skipped from Norway ahead of the Hun and sailed as a trooper for the rest of the war. She had a small British staff (medic and disciplinary) and though under British orders, flew the Norwegian flag. Her crew were very proud of this! We were made much of by the Norwegians and British trooper staff – you would think we were long lost mates come home. We ate ship's bread (white, would you believe it?) like cake and stuffed ourselves at every meal, with the inevitable result – but it was worth it! We waited until more men came through, then at noon on May 3 we sailed. A wonderful sight – the strip of water between ship and wharf widening and widening. It was no dream – at last we were with our own.

Eric Laker and his fellow prisoners finally embarked from their work camp at Lindau at lunchtime on 20 May 1945. For the first time they were able to witness life outside their camp in the towns and cities en route and noted, in particular, the destruction caused by the Allied bombing. He would eventually fly back to England from Reims.

A great many Lancasters on the 'drome and we boarded one at 4.15pm. One engine failed to start however and we had to wait an hour and a half while repairs were done. We were dancing round with impatience and I almost got to biting my fingernails. All other planes had gone and we finally took off at 6.05pm, arriving at

Oakley at 7.50pm. A fairly smooth journey, part of which I made in the mid-ships air turret. Great fun moving the guns up and down and spinning the turret round. When we landed at Oakley we trooped into a hangar with tables set out containing stacks of food. Everybody however was, I believe, too full up with excitement to eat much. I know I was. A great placard was hanging up bearing the words 'Welcome Home', but I am afraid I could not see it very well. My eyes were too misty. The kindness of these people seems to get you somehow. An end to bombing and barbed wire, guns and Germans. It seems much too good to be true that it is all over, that I am in England again at last.

On finally reaching home, ex-prisoners of war were each given six weeks of special repatriation leave, during which they were expected to attend a full medical examination. After being demobilised, each man was also given the opportunity to attend a Civil Resettlement Unit if he wished to. These were residential units intended to bridge the gap between prisoner of war and civilian life. Many ex-prisoners struggled to re-establish themselves back home. Many years spent experiencing inadequate amounts of food had a long-term effect on Stanley Doughty, which continued to be felt for many years after his liberation.

I just cannot leave anything on my plate. I would rather be uncomfortably full than do so. Moreover it distresses me when others do so, even though it may go to feed the animals... Waste of any sort, but particularly of food, grieves me to the point of actually hurting, and I will go to any lengths, however absurd, to avoid it.

Having been captured at Tobruk in June 1942, Corporal Harvey ended up spending almost three years as a prisoner of war. Finally liberated, a Dakota aircraft transported him as far as a French channel port, from where he would then finish the journey by ferry to

Dover where a warm reception awaited. The next morning he started off for Doncaster, and home. To see his wife and children again after such a long time must have been an extremely emotional occasion.

So there I was walking down Chequer Avenue to Edith and the children, I know we were liberated about the middle of May and here I was. One thing struck me as I walked. The march I have described started on January 15th 1945 in Brzeg and we were liberated in the middle of May which meant we were walking the highways of Germany for four months and in that time I don't recall receiving any other hot food, like soup or potatoes, only the pitiful bread ration. In retrospect it seems unbelievable that we could have survived the ordeal. I walked into the kitchen and as usual in these precious moments there was a nosey neighbour evidently wanting to be in the reunion, the first time I had seen Edith since January 1942. Janet the little toddler I had left was now about 8/9 years and the baby Billie who I last saw in a pram was now a little boy of 5/6 years. I remember kissing Edith but after that time apart we both felt rather strange with each other and I suppose in my rundown condition I would seem aloof and miserable. It was at least a fortnight before we could come together in the normal relationship of husband and wife, due entirely to my physical condition.

Following the various reunions with family and friends, the sudden novelty of decent meals and a warm bed, many prisoners of war found themselves experiencing a degree of bitterness towards their wartime experience. Many felt that their time in captivity had been a waste and that they had a lot of catching up to do in the way of careers and life in general; others felt frustration that their contribution to the war effort had not been seen in the same way as those members of the liberating armies who were themselves now starting to come home to great acclaim. Corporal Harvey's demobilisation group was due for discharge at the beginning of

November 1945 and on that day he reported to barracks to receive his demob outfit and final payment.

The total was £130 which may have seemed a lot in that day and age, until I started work and found a lot of workmen already had more than that in post war tax credits... It struck me as we occasionally walked through the town not a soul spoke to us. I suppose after the glamour of Americans, Free French and Polish troops we were just nondescripts. Our pleasure of being home and survival did not seem to have universal appeal, and my thoughts were somewhat bitter.

There was a common belief among returning prisoners that civilians back on the home front or service personnel who had served in active campaigns would be unable or unwilling to appreciate the nature of their experiences in captivity. This notion was similar to the bitterness felt by many First World War soldiers when the harsh warfare of the trenches contrasted with the jingoistic ideas of those at home. Lieutenant Harwood, whose prisoner of war experiences are described throughout this book, wrote a memoir some years after the conflict in which he declared the intention of recording to the best of his ability what prisoner of war life was truly like.

On returning to England I met a number of people who seemed interested in, and extremely ignorant of, the conditions and treatment in the various prison camps. Their ideas varied enormously; some imagined that we had lived in comfort and even luxury, free to do as we pleased and go where we wished; others visualised a sort of 'Belsen' existence. Both conceptions were very wide of the mark. I decided to attempt a rough picture of the facts as I saw them.

It is to the credit of Lieutenant Harwood and so many other prisoners of war that they chose to document their experiences in this way, ensuring that their testimony could inform future generations. The privations they had experienced in captivity, such as poor food, ill health, mistreatment and an overall very low standard of living, were endured on behalf of their nation. The long-term effect of their captivity, both on themselves and their immediate family and friends, should not be underestimated. Through the sharing of experiences and the wider public understanding of their plight, ex-prisoners of war would come to realise that rather than being forgotten, their contribution to the Second World War would become increasingly recognised as an incredibly valuable and much appreciated one.

Image List

Documents.684, HU 9210, Documents.2188/A, EPH 9976, Documents.13456/B, Documents.19672/B, HU 20930, HU 47237 © the rights holder, HU 21013, COM 504, HU 9213, HU 9265, ART LD 5155, HU 9274, HU 47180, HU 20945, HU 47084 © the rights holder, HU 47156 © the rights holder, HU 47107 © the rights holder, HU 49544, HU 49551, HU 109911 © New Zealand Crown Copyright / Imperial War Museum, HU 49532, BU 5985, BU 6001, BU 3661

Sources

IWM DOCUMENTS

© IWM unless otherwise stated

Private Papers of S J Doughty
(Documents.3189)
Private Papers of E G Laker
(Documents.3576)
Private Papers of K T Clarke
(Documents.9990)
Private Papers of Captain E Monckton
(Documents.3653)
Private Papers of Flight Lieutenant E E
Williams (Documents.4077)
Private Papers of T Tateson
(Documents.1784)
Private Papers of W G Harvey
(Documents.9623)
Oliver Philpot quoted in the Private
Papers of Flight Lieutenant E E Williams
(Documents.4077)
Private Papers of 2nd Lieutenant F J Stewart
(Documents.1054)
Report by CSM James Fulton held
in the Private Papers of N R Wylie
(Documents.4228)
Private Papers of E Randolph
(Documents.3504)

Private Papers of W Sutton
(Documents.19274)
Private Papers of H C F Harwood
(Documents.3971)
Private Papers of A Bolt (Documents.17610)
Private Papers of N R Wylie
(Documents.4228)
Private Papers of Lieutenant Colonel E J A
H Brush (Documents.3525)
Private Papers of Squadron Leader R J
Bushell (Documents.21101)
Private Papers of Lieutenant Colonel
M Reid, letter of 26 September 1943
(Documents.4275)
MI9 interim debriefing report of Flight
Lieutenant H N Fowler, held within
Private Papers of Lieutenant L A Wingfield
(IWM Documents.18776)
Private Papers of Dr R Eggers
(Documents.1805)
Private Papers of Major H G Bruce
(Documents.6295)
Private Papers of E Randolph (IWM
Documents.3504)

PUBLICATIONS

Adrian Gilbert, *P.O.W.: Allied Prisoners in Europe, 1939–1945*, John Murray, 2006

Neville Wylie, *Barbed Wire Diplomacy: Britain, Germany and the Politics of Prisoners of War 1939–1945*, Oxford University Press, 2010

Clare Makepeace, *Captives of War: British Prisoners of War in Europe in the Second World War*, Cambridge University Press, 2017

Midge Gillies, *The Barbed-Wire University: The Real Lives of Prisoners of War in the Second World War*, Aurum Press Ltd, 2011

M.R.D. Foot and J.M. Langley, *MI 9: Escape and Evasion 1939–1945*, Bodley Head, 1979

Arthur A Durand, *Stalag Luft III: The Secret Story*, Louisiana State University Press, 1988

Hansard, accessed at https://api.parliament.uk/historic-hansard/commons/1945/may/29/british-prisoners-of-war-repatriation [March 2019]

Henry Chancellor, *Colditz: The Definitive History*, Hodder & Stoughton, 2001

IWM SOUND ARCHIVE

Patrick Welch (10643)
Francis Edwards (17597)